Watchable Birds of
CALIFORNIA

Mary Taylor Gray

Photographs by **Herbert Clarke**

Mountain Press Publishing Company
Missoula, Montana
1999

Library of Congress Cataloging-in-Publication Data
Gray, Mary Taylor, 1955–
    Watchable birds of California / Mary Taylor Gray ;
photographs by Herbert Clarke.
        p. cm.
    Includes bibliographical references (p.   ) and index.
    ISBN 0-87842-389-3 (alk. paper)
    1. Birds—California. 2. Bird watching—California. I.
Clarke, Herbert, 1927– . II. Title.
QL684.C2G746 1998
598'.09794—dc21   98-47307
                                                       CIP

PRINTED IN HONG KONG BY MANTEC PRODUCTION COMPANY

Mountain Press Publishing Company
1301 S. Third Street W. • P. O. Box 2399
Missoula, Montana 59806
406-728-1900

To my bright and beautiful daughter, Olivia,
who came into the world not long before this book,
and who reminds me every day what really matters in life.
—M. T. G.

To Olga—you are the wind beneath my wings!
—H. C.

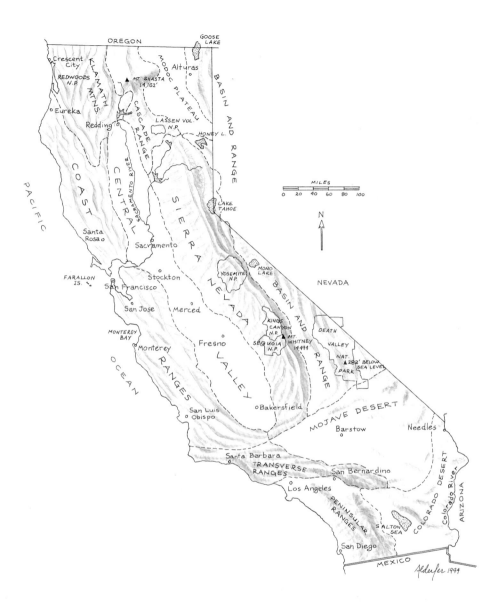

CONTENTS

Birds of Freshwater:
Rivers, Lakes, Marshes, and Streamside Woodlands   61

ACKNOWLEDGMENTS

Many thanks to Herb and Olga Clarke for their help and support as we brought this union to fruition. Thanks also to Jim Peugh and Claude G. Edwards of the San Diego Audubon Society for help with questions. And thanks to Deb Long and my husband, Richard Young, who were my birding companions. I am especially grateful to the wonderful birds, who shared their beauty and their secrets.

—M. T. G.

❖

Over the years, I have been the fortunate recipient of good advice, companionship, encouragement, and luck from many people and other sources while pursuing the work I enjoy most—photographing birds in the wild. There are far too many colleagues to enumerate, so I collectively thank those friends here. Of course, my main pillar has been my wife, Olga, whose shining light has guided me through many difficult situations. Again, as with previous books, the staff at Mountain Press Publishing Company, under the direction of Kathleen Ort, have been outstanding in their cooperation and understanding of my many requests in editing and arrangement of this book.

—H. C.

City of Los Angeles

Tufa towers at Mono Lake

INTRODUCTION

California is a wonderland of birds. The diversity and richness of natural habitats across California's 101 million acres are unrivaled in the United States. The state ranges in elevation from 14,495-foot Mount Whitney to Death Valley at 282 feet below sea level. Within California's borders are ocean beaches, redwood forests, crashing sea cliffs, desert palm oases, lush meadows, offshore islands, grasslands, salt marshes, teeming tidepools, and dry desert washes. For all this natural abundance and diversity, California has been described as an island, a world apart, a separate land. Despite the vast development of California's wild lands for human use, its many ecosystems remain a veritable cornucopia of birds.

Almost 600 bird species have been recorded in California, birds of all shapes, sizes, families, and lifestyles. This book will not attempt to look at all of them—many fine existing bird guides already do that. Rather, *Watchable Birds of California* is a "birder's choice," focusing on a selection of birds that are especially fun and interesting to observe because they are particularly big or small, unique in appearance, brightly colored, or have fascinating behaviors. In other words, they're "watchable."

Watchable birds aren't necessarily the most common birds, but neither are they so rare or hard to spot that only dedicated birders will find them. All the birds profiled here can be seen by novice birdwatchers with a little study, some effort, and good binoculars.

Watchable Birds of California, like its predecessors, *Watchable Birds of the Rocky Mountains* and *Watchable Birds of the Southwest,* is geared for families, tourists, nature lovers, armchair naturalists, and anyone who enjoys birds and the outdoors. The text is written to help readers enjoy birds and get to know a bit of the character of each species. Readers will discover fun and intriguing tidbits about the "private lives" of the birds that are so much a part of the California outdoors. *Watchable Birds* can be a helpful companion to a field guide or stand alone as enjoyable reading. For some it may be a first step toward an interest in birdwatching, for others a source for basic information and interesting facts on birds of the region.

HOW TO USE THIS BOOK

Traditional field guides are grouped taxonomically by family. But most novice birdwatchers are not versed in the family groupings of bird species. They may know a woodpecker from a duck but not a warbler from a flycatcher. *Watchable Birds of California* is organized into four very broad habitat groupings—Seacoast, Freshwater, Open Country, and High Country—that are readily apparent to even the most casual visitor. While novice naturalists may not recognize coastal sage scrub or a ponderosa-pine montane forest, they do know if they are along the ocean or up in the mountains. Readers need only note which general habitat they are visiting, then look within that section of the book for the bird they wish to read about. For simplicity's sake, the book assigns each species to the habitat it most typically inhabits. But birds are highly mobile; many don't frequent these habitats exclusively, so don't be surprised to see some of these birds showing up in other places, particularly as seasonal changes bring them from summer nesting grounds to wintering sites.

Seacoast: Beaches, Bays, Estuaries, Salt Marshes, Sea Cliffs, and Open Ocean

The California coastline is home to a host of wonderful and amazing birds. Some spend their life at sea; others patrol the beach or comb rocky cliffs and shorelines. Many birds prefer the gentler conditions of salt marshes and bays or the mixed waters of an estuary. The Seacoast habitat grouping encompasses the many saltwater communities found at and near the ocean. Though not at the coast, the highly saline Salton Sea hosts many of the birds found in this grouping.

Freshwater: Rivers, Lakes, Marshes, and Streamside Woodlands

Many species of birds live near freshwater—those like waterfowl and wading birds that actually live on or in the water and others that live near water because of the abundant food resources associated with it. The Freshwater habitat grouping encompasses rivers, lakes, reservoirs, freshwater marshes, streams, sloughs, irrigation ditches and canals, ponds, and other wetland and riparian communities.

Open Country: Deserts, Grasslands, Chaparral, and Farmland

Much of California's terrain, including vast agricultural lands, is not heavily forested, mountainous, or dominated by water. The various open-terrain communities of grasslands, chaparral, scrub- and shrublands, deserts, farm fields, rangeland, and savanna (open land with scattered trees) comprise the Open Country habitat grouping.

High Country: Mountains, Canyons, and Forests

In summer the lush mountains of California offer abundant resources for many birds—flowering plants, nuts, seeds, berries, insects, small mammals, as well as protected nesting sites. Many birds found in higher elevations and northern habitats in summer move into lower and more southerly areas in winter. The High Country habitat grouping includes mountain meadows, forests, alpine tundra, canyons, mountain valleys, and coastal forests.

Anatomy of a Species Profile

Size: A graphic scale with a vertical bar indicates the size of each species in relation to silhouettes of familiar birds. Because the shapes and postures of birds vary so much, and affect our perception of size, two different silhouette scales are used: one for land birds and one for waterbirds. These silhouettes are not drawn in accurate proportion to one another, but merely ranked from smallest to largest. These size scales more closely reflect body size and shape than overall length from tip of outstretched bill to end of tail, the usual method of measuring bird size.

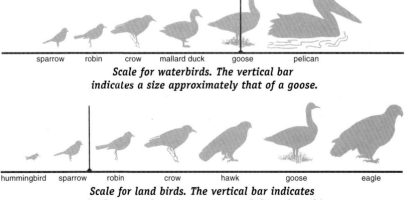

sparrow　robin　crow　mallard duck　goose　pelican
Scale for waterbirds. The vertical bar indicates a size approximately that of a goose.

hummingbird　sparrow　robin　crow　hawk　goose　eagle
Scale for land birds. The vertical bar indicates a size between that of a sparrow and that of a robin.

Shorebirds

Name: Birds are listed by the American Ornithologists' Union (A.O.U.) accepted common name, per the seventh edition of the A.O.U. checklist, followed by the two-part scientific or Latin name, shown in *italics*. Subspecies are referenced within the text, where appropriate.

Family: This references the family group of each profiled bird.

A.K.A. (Also Known As): This lists other common and colloquial names that may be more familiar to readers than the "official" common name.

Eye-catchers: This calls attention to particular features or behaviors that help distinguish a species from other birds.

Description: A brief physical description of the bird follows the name and family information. Where adult males and females differ in appearance, both are described. Winter plumages are described for species commonly wintering in California. With a few exceptions, juvenile plumages are not described, being beyond the scope of this book.

Natural History: This offers information on the species' life history, behavior, folklore, and other fun and interesting tidbits. Related or similar species are indicated in **bold.**

When and Where to See Them: This describes the geographic area and habitats each bird inhabits in California at various times of year.

HOW TO IDENTIFY BIRDS

Watching birds is lots more fun if you can identify them. A bird flits by, and you think you noticed enough detail to identify it, but upon checking your bird guide you find several different species that seem to match the bird you saw. Training yourself to make a few mental notes when you glimpse a bird will help improve your identification success.

Size. It can be difficult to accurately judge the size of a bird at any distance. Try instead to judge a bird's size in relation to other familiar birds. Is it about the size of a sparrow? Is it bigger than a robin but smaller than a crow? This book indicates size in relation to familiar birds on a silhouette chart.

Shape. What is the bird's general shape? Is it round and chunky like a sparrow or slender like a mockingbird? Take note of the shape of body parts. Are the wings long and pointed or short and rounded? Is the tail long or cocked up? Is the bill short and sturdy for cracking seeds or slender and sharp for grabbing insects? These characteristics will help you make some general associations and differentiate between similar birds. Within the raptor family, for example, falcons have slender, tapering wings for fast pursuit in the air; open-country hawks have large, wide wings for soaring; and woodland hawks have short, rounded wings for maneuvering among trees.

Field Marks. Sometimes you have only a moment to glimpse a bird. Watch for noticeable features—distinctive stripes, colors, and patterns. Is the breast spotted, are there stripes over the eyes, or white edges to the tail? Do patches under the wings or on the tail "flash" when the bird flies? You may notice a crest, but is it pointed like a cardinal's or more sloping like a kingfisher's?

Behavior. Notice the bird's activities. Is it gripping the trunk of a tree and pecking at the bark like a woodpecker? Does it fly out from a perch, make a loop in the air, and sail back to the same perch in typical flycatcher style? Does it dive underwater or bob on the water's surface and reach below for food?

Voice. Birdsong fills the natural world with life and joyful music. Becoming familiar with birdsong is not only a pleasure but a clue to what birds are in the neighborhood, even when they are hidden from view. Begin by learning easy and common bird voices, like the *cheer-up* of the robin or the California quail's *chi-CA-go*. Listening to tapes of birdsongs, available in bookstores and wild bird shops, will help improve your skills.

Habitat. Where a bird lives provides clues to its identity. You'll obviously know if you're in a woodland rather than a meadow, but is the forest dense or open? Is it dominated by conifers or deciduous trees? Begin to associate certain habitats with certain birds. Do you always see a certain bird near water?

TIPS FOR BETTER BIRDWATCHING

- Binoculars are an essential tool for birdwatching. They come in all prices and levels of quality, so learn all you can, then buy the best you can afford. Wait to invest in a spotting scope. Scopes are wonderful tools for birding but also expensive and cumbersome and generally not a good idea for beginners.

- Time your outings for when birds are most active—the hours around dawn and dusk. You will have the least success during the middle of the day.

Mass of dowitchers and other shorebirds

- Come prepared. Dress in layers so you can stay comfortable as a cool morning heats up. Remember to bring a hat, sunscreen, water, sturdy footwear, and raingear.

- Wear neutral colors such as gray, khaki, or olive green to help you blend into the surroundings. Birds see color very well, and white or brightly colored shirts stand out like flags.

- Don't march directly up to a bird; it will most likely flee. Instead, approach quietly and indirectly, stopping occasionally to look through your binoculars.

- Listen for calls, and watch for shapes and movement. If you spot a bird, keep your eyes on it and bring your binoculars up into your line of sight.

- Try different watching modes. You can keep on the move searching for birds, or sit quietly in one spot and observe the activity that blossoms around you.

BIRDWATCHING ETHICS AND ETIQUETTE

- Birdwatching is a wonderful hobby, but it also carries responsibilities. When watching birds, remember that you are entering the animals' "home" and should conduct yourself as a guest.

- Respect the birds and don't disturb them, their young, their nests, or their habitat. Intrusion into a bird's living space can expose it to predation, keep it from feeding, or cause it to leave or abandon its nest, exposing eggs or chicks to predation or the elements. No sighting or photo is worth stressing or endangering birds.

- Don't approach any closer than the birds feel comfortable. If they alter their behavior, stop feeding, or otherwise seem agitated, back off. If a bird flushes or flies off, you won't get a very good look anyway.

- Never chase, feed, handle, or disturb birds or wildlife.

- Leave your pets at home.

- Respect the rights of landowners and don't enter private property without permission.

- When in parks or on public land, respect the rules.

Rocky coast near Trinidad

Coast near San Simeon with elephant seal in right foreground

BIRDS OF THE SEACOAST
Beaches, Bays, Estuaries, Salt Marshes, Sea Cliffs, and Open Ocean

Common Loon
Western Grebe/Clark's Grebe
Black-footed Albatross/
   Pink-footed Shearwater/
   Pigeon Guillemot
Brown Pelican
Brandt's Cormorant
Northern Pintail
Surf Scoter
Red-breasted Merganser/
   Common Merganser
Osprey
Clapper Rail
Black-bellied Plover/
   Semipalmated Plover/Snowy Plover

Black Oystercatcher
Black-necked Stilt
American Avocet
Willet
Whimbrel
Long-billed Curlew
Marbled Godwit
Black Turnstone
Sanderling/Least Sandpiper
Short-billed Dowitcher/
   Long-billed Dowitcher
Wilson's Phalarope
Heermann's Gull/Western Gull
Forster's Tern/Least Tern
Black Skimmer

COMMON LOON

Gavia immer
Family: Loons
A.K.A.: walloon, big loon, call-up-a-storm

Eye-catchers: The loon's low-rider swimming profile, long straight bill, and very level head posture define it on the water.

A large waterbird that rides low in the water, in winter plumage the loon has a dark gray back, nape, and crown with a white throat and breast. In summer the body bears a striking pattern of pearly white squares and speckles on black, with white streaking on the neck, a black neck band, greenish head, and red eye.

Natural History: Loons are the legendary water ghosts of the lake country of the northern states and Canada, their eerie, laughing calls echoing like tremulous human voices in the mist. California hosts these birds in winter, when they flee cold northern waters for the seacoast. In winter, loons seem to be traveling incognito; they are generally silent and have lost their distinctive summer plumage, replaced by nondescript white and dark gray. Loons sometimes appear in summer plumage in California, especially early migrating birds.

A raft of loons bobbing on the waters of a bay is a fascinating sight. Loons are premier waterbirds and fishers, built like avian submarines. They will suddenly disappear out of sight as they dive after fish, chasing them down underwater. A loon's legs are located far back on the body, well-designed to provide underwater propulsion. While most birds have light, hollow bones, the loon's bones are denser, nearly the same as the specific gravity of water. This lessens the bird's buoyancy and allows it to submerge efficiently. Never tell a loon "don't hold your breath"; these birds have been timed underwater for up to three minutes. They can reach great depth in their dives and have been recorded in the Great Lakes at depths of 600 feet. In flight, the loon holds its big "paddle feet" out behind like a pair of shipped oars. These large feet, along with the common loon's large size, angular head, and long straight bill, help distinguish it from other loons, all of which are quite similar in winter plumage.

When and Where to See Them: October to April on seacoasts, bays, and harbors the length of the state. On larger interior lakes during migration and in winter.

Common Loon in winter plumage

Common Loon in breeding plumage

WESTERN GREBE

Aechmophorus occidentalis
Family: Grebes
A.K.A.: swan grebe, western dabchick

Eye-catchers: The western grebe rides so low in the water at times that only its curving, swanlike, black-and-white neck is visible, looking like a snake arching up out of the water.

This swan-necked grebe is distinctively two-toned, with black back, neck, and crown in contrast to a white chin, throat, and undersides. It has a greenish yellow bill and red eye.

Natural History: The genus name for the western grebe—*Aechmophorus*—means "spear-bearer," an apt description, for this bird's long, slender, sharply pointed bill enables it to pluck fish and other prey from the water. Watching a grebe is a game of "now you see him, now you don't" as the bird, sailing serenely on the surface one minute, suddenly ducks underwater, only to pop up again unpredictably somewhere else.

While western grebes are winter birds along the California coast, many also spend summer nesting on inland lakes. In spring one of the highlights of nature is the courtship dance of the western grebe, a real treat should you happen to witness a pair on their nesting waters. The dance begins as a male and female swim together on the water, bobbing their heads and exchanging a screechy *kree-eek* call. Then the two swim toward each other, entwining their necks as they pirouette slowly on the water. Side by side they swim, each arching its neck back gracefully as if acknowledging the other's importance. Finally, in a dramatic climax, the two suddenly rise up on the water and scamper across the surface together in a flurry of splashing.

As with loons and other diving waterbirds, the legs of the grebe are set far back on its body, which enhances underwater swimming but makes walking almost impossible. Thus grebes are rarely seen on land, and since they are indifferent fliers, not often in flight. Grebes build floating nests of aquatic vegetation, which they anchor to cattail stalks. Once the young hatch they climb aboard their parents' backs, holding on with their bills to the adults' feathers when the parents dive.

The **Clark's grebe** is quite similar to the western grebe, but distinguish it by its bright orange yellow bill, as opposed to the greenish bill of the western grebe. The black on the head of Clark's grebe also usually stops above the eye.

When and Where to See Them: Along the coast and on large bays in winter as well as on the Salton Sea. Mid-May to September on large inland lakes.

Western Grebe

Clark's Grebe

BLACK-FOOTED ALBATROSS

Phoebastria nigripes
Family: Albatrosses
A.K.A.: gooney bird, black gooney

Eye-catchers: You will only see this bird from a boat, so watch for a very large, dark bird with a bulbous head and heavy, hooked bill. If one passes close overhead you may mistake it for a small aircraft.

This huge, gull-like bird with very long wings is grayish black with a white face and dark brown bill.

Natural History: Imagine staying at sea most of your life, soaring above the waves, settling to the water only to feed or when there is insufficient wind to keep you aloft, and coming to land only briefly to nest. Such is the incredible life history of the albatross. Without Samuel Coleridge's classic poem "The Rime of the Ancient Mariner," whose main character was doomed to wear an albatross about his neck as penance, most of us would probably never have heard of this sea-dwelling bird, and very few of us will ever see one. Along with shearwaters, petrels, fulmars, and a few other birds, albatrosses are pelagic birds, meaning they stay at sea nearly their entire lives and are rarely sighted from land. Take a boat trip off the coast, however, and you may well see an albatross. They have learned to follow fishing boats to feed on the offal and garbage thrown overboard. Albatrosses are distinguished from gulls, petrels, and other similar birds by their great size. The albatross's amazingly long, narrow wings allow it to ride the air currents above the ocean most of its life. Albatrosses can also drink seawater. A tubular device atop the bill (for which they are dubbed "tube noses") houses a salt-excreting gland through which they excrete a highly concentrated salt solution that allows the birds to eliminate the excess salt they consume.

Albatrosses require 10 to 12 years to reach maturity. They come to land only to nest in large colonies on remote atolls near the Hawaiian Islands and others in the central Pacific. The albatross pair is said to mate for life, the female laying a single egg in a shallow scrape in the sand about every other year. Once the young albatross leaves the nest it may be nine years before the bird returns to land.

Other pelagic birds you may see if boating off the California coast include the **pink-footed shearwater,** a summer visitor, and the **pigeon guillemot,** which breeds on islets and mainland cliffs along the central coast.

When and Where to See Them: On open ocean mainly off central California coasts through most of the year, peaking in summer. Often follows boats and ships.

Black-footed Albatross

Pink-footed Shearwater

Pigeon Guillemot in breeding plumage

BROWN PELICAN

Pelecanus occidentalis
Family: Pelicans
A.K.A.: common pelican

Eye-catchers: Watch for lines of huge pelicans flying in formation above the waves, alternately flapping and gliding. The long, pouched bill belongs only to the pelican.

This very large seabird is grayish brown with a yellowish white head and dark belly. The bill is very long with a large pouch that lies flat unless filled with water while feeding. During summer the back of the adult's neck becomes dark chestnut and a red patch appears on the throat.

Natural History: What at first appears to be a patrol of small aircraft flying in a line just above the waves becomes, upon closer inspection, a group of brown pelicans. These very large birds—their wingspan reaches seven and one-half feet—are a delight to watch, with unusual bills, methodical flight, and dramatic fishing style. Pelicans fly in formation, heads folded back against their bodies, pouches tucked beneath their bills, all flapping together slowly and solemnly.

While the freshwater-favoring white pelican sits on the water's surface sedately dipping fish from the water with its pouched bill, the brown pelican uses a more aggressive fishing style. Spotting a fish in the water while patrolling from the air, it dives headfirst into the waves, sometimes from a height of 60 feet. With this momentum it can nab prey at greater depths than its cousin. The brown pelican may submerge completely or only partially, depending on the height of the dive, coming up with a pouch full of fish that it gulps down while bobbing on the water. The pelican is equipped with safety flotation devices—air sacs beneath the skin that bob the bird immediately to the surface after a dive. It always comes up facing into the wind and ready to take off again.

Brown pelican populations were dramatically affected by eggshell thinning from pesticides the birds picked up through the food chain by feeding in polluted coastal waters. In 1969 only five young were raised in California. Through intense recovery efforts the pelican, immortalized in Dixon Merritt's limerick as a bird "whose bill will hold more than his belican," has recovered somewhat and is now commonly seen along the coast, though it remains an endangered species.

When and Where to See Them: On open seas, bays, estuaries, and harbors along southern California coasts year-round and farther north midsummer through fall. Also on the Salton Sea mainly in summer.

Brown Pelican

BRANDT'S CORMORANT

Phalacrocorax penicillatus
Family: Cormorants
A.K.A.: brown cormorant, shag, penciled cormorant

Eye-catchers: Typically "cormorant-esque" in its posture and flight profile, the Brandt's is distinguished from other cormorants by the blue throat of the adults.

This sea-dwelling cormorant has black plumage and a buffy chin patch. Breeding adults have a bright blue skin pouch beneath the bill.

Natural History: Brandt's cormorants often gather in tight groups to feed, bobbing on the ocean like so many black periscopes with only their heads and necks visible above the waves. Highly gregarious, a large group of them clustered together looks like a bunch of "sea crows," a common nickname. They nest in island colonies and frequently fly in long lines or wedges. Brandt's often mingle with other cormorant species, and marinas and docks lined with their long-necked forms offer a chance to compare the species variations among these rather similar birds.

Cormorants are strong fliers and powerful divers. Once underwater they hold their wings out as if gliding and kick strongly with their webbed feet. To reduce buoyancy they have heavy bones and small air sacs and can compress their feathers to squeeze out pockets of air. Their feathers are not waterproof like those of a duck—another adaptation for diving—thus, when a cormorant finishes fishing it must leave the water and dry its feathers. A classic cormorant pose is with the wings held out to dry, like an angel posed with outstretched wings.

When and Where to See Them: Year-round the length of the state along the coast on cliffs, breakwaters, harbors.

Brandt's Cormorant

Flock of Brandt's Cormorants

NORTHERN PINTAIL

Anas acuta
Family: Swans, geese, and ducks
A.K.A.: sprig tail, pheasant duck, picket-tail

Eye-catchers: Like an arrow pointing straight to him, the male pintail's "pin tail" points him out in a crowd.

The male pintail is a handsome, bronze brown duck with a dramatic white stripe on each side of the head and neck. The body is mottled gray brown with several long, pointed feathers protruding at an angle from the tail. The female is a drab, mottled brown.

Natural History: Pintails are dabbling ducks. To feed they tip "bottoms up" in shallow water, reaching down to sift snails, insects, and the seeds of aquatic plants from the mud on the lake bottom. This feeding strategy led to significant mortality among pintail populations due to lead poisoning from ingestion of spent shotgun pellets in the mud. With the requirement for steel shot, the outlook for all affected species of waterfowl is improving, but at one time as many as 3 million ducks, geese, and other waterfowl were estimated to die of lead poisoning annually.

Pintails move into California from northern nesting grounds in late summer, inhabiting coastal bays and estuaries and gathering in huge numbers on the wetlands and lakes of the Central Valley. The most abundant species of wintering waterfowl in the state, pintail numbers may boom to an astounding 3 million ducks at their winter peak. A few remain in spring to nest, mainly in the Klamath and Great Basins. Pintails are particularly sociable with another abundant dabbling duck, the mallard, and the two species are often seen together and may occasionally interbreed.

Pintails select their mates in late fall and the pair spends winter together, offering California birdwatchers the opportunity to observe their courtship behavior. After mating in spring, the male leaves the female to incubate the eggs and rear the young. If danger threatens the nest, the female may feign injury like a killdeer to lead predators away from the nest.

When and Where to See Them: From late summer through April on saltwater bays, estuaries, and lagoons and freshwater lakes, ponds, and marshes throughout the state. Large concentrations on northern lakes in fall and Central Valley lakes and wetlands in winter.

Northern Pintail male

Northern Pintail feeding

SURF SCOTER
Melanitta perspicillata
Family: Swans, geese, and ducks
A.K.A.: goggle-nose, surfer, skunk duck

Eye-catchers: You can't miss the male surf scoter's colorful bill.

The male is black with white patches on its forehead and nape and an oversized bill colored white, yellow, and red. The drab brown female has the same bloated bill but hers lacks color; she has two white spots on each side of her head.

Natural History: As you watch a line of surf scoters bobbing on the water of a bay, you may see the first in line suddenly arch up and dive under the surface. A moment later the next in line dives, then a moment later the next, then the next. The entire line of scoters dives in sequence, as if each duck is diving through the same hole in the water. At other times a great raft of scoters swimming together may all suddenly dive together, disappearing at the same moment as if one of them had been calling out, "Ready, set, dive!"

Surf scoters are so named for their habit of feeding just beyond the breaking surf, "scooting" through the breakers. They dive as deep as 30 feet to feed on mussels, clams, periwinkles, crabs, and other marine life. Underwater, the scoter propels itself with its feet and partially opened wings. A knob of feathers that protrudes from the first digit of the wing like a thumb acts as a stabilizer.

The surf scoter is among the most striking and interesting of ducks, not because of its beauty but because of its big schnoz—a bulbous bill brightly colored in bold contrast to its black plumage.

Scoters court in winter, allowing us a good chance to watch their antics. A group of males gathers around a prospective female, the male ducks gurgling and whistling and darting after each other as they chase the female. Finally the whole group dives, and when they come up the female has made her choice.

In spring most surf scoters depart California for nesting grounds on Canada's northern tundra. Before long they will be back on California coastal waters for winter. Luckily for birdwatchers, unlike some ducks, scoters do not change into drab winter plumage (except their first year), remaining colorful throughout the year.

When and Where to See Them: October to May along seacoasts the length of the state at bays, harbors, estuaries, and lagoons.

Surf Scoter males displaying to female

Surf Scoter male

RED-BREASTED MERGANSER

Mergus serrator
Family: Swans, geese, and ducks
A.K.A.: sea robin, fuzzyhead, sawbill

Eye-catchers: The male's green head and raggedy crest identify him, as does the typical merganser bill—long, hooked, and very flat on the underside.

The male is gray with a black back, rusty red breast, white neck ring, and green head with a rough crest. The female is gray brown with a rusty head and her own tattered-looking crest.

Natural History: Mergansers look rather different from their more familiar cousins, the dabbling ducks. At a distance it's easy to tell a merganser because of its long, thin bill, which appears very straight and flat on the underside. In flight the narrow head is held out so straight one might almost take a ruler to trace the flat, even line under the bill and neck. Mergansers usually fly low and single file above the water. "Merganser" means diving goose, a reference to these ducks' large size. The British call them "goosanders," meaning goose-duck.

Mergansers are consummate divers. Their legs are located toward the back of their bodies, providing strong paddling and propulsion underwater. Their bills have a characteristic hook and serrated edges to help them hold their slippery prey, which is primarily fish. At times mergansers gather in great rafts of birds, and it is comical to watch them all snorkeling along together, bills poking into the water seeking prey. Red-breasted mergansers sometimes form skirmish lines, a flock of them swimming abreast herding fish toward shallow water where the fish are more easily caught.

A red-breasted can be distinguished from its cousin the **common merganser** by its colored breast and ragged, punkish crest. Though both have green heads, the common merganser's head is smooth and its breast snowy white.

When and Where to See Them: The length of California from October to May on saltwater bays, lagoons, and estuaries. During migration on freshwater inland lakes.

Red-breasted Merganser male

Common Merganser male

OSPREY

Pandion haliaetus
Family: Hawks and eagles
A.K.A.: fish eagle, fish hawk

Eye-catchers: The osprey's white head with a roguish line of black streaked through the eye and across the head, and its hunting strategy of flying low over open water, distinguish it from other raptors.

This large hawk with charcoal back and wings has a white head and breast. A black eye stripe passes down the side of the head. In flight, watch for black wrist patches on the undersides of the white wings.

Natural History: To witness an osprey strike the water and come up with a glistening fish writhing in its talons is to see a true display of fierce and wild nature. This beautifully marked bird of prey lives almost exclusively on fish, hunting open waters with a fierce and watchful eye, striking with great power and speed once it spots a silvery body in the water below. Locating prey, the osprey begins its powerful dive, rocking its legs forward as it nears the water, then slashing with its talons. Sometimes this big fish hawk can seize its quarry and lift into the air again without entering the water, but just as often it takes a bath, splashing in the water as it struggles to overpower its prey, which can be a good-size fish. With powerful wing beats the osprey lifts from the water. Once aloft the bird will turn the fish it carries so the head is facing forward, a behavioral adaptation to reduce wind resistance during flight.

Ospreys are fish eaters at the top of the food chain, and like bald eagles they have suffered eggshell thinning from DDT pesticide (little fish eats plant contaminated with DDT, is eaten by bigger fish, which is eaten by bigger fish, which is eaten by osprey, with the poison concentrating at each step). Osprey populations have also suffered from shooting and loss of their wetlands habitat but are making a recovery after strong conservation efforts, including the construction of nesting platforms at appropriate sites. At one time ospreys were fairly common nesters in California, but now only about 400 pairs nest in the state, primarily around lakes in northern California.

When and Where to See Them: Fall through spring along seacoasts all along the state. In summer on northern mountain lakes.

Osprey

Osprey in flight

CLAPPER RAIL

Rallus longirostris
Family: Rails and coots
A.K.A.: Yuma rail, light-footed rail, sedge hen

Eye-catchers: A stealthy bird glowing copper in the sun, the clapper feeds at the edge of vegetation in cordgrass or pickleweed salt marshes.

This large rail has a fairly long, somewhat down-curved bill and an overall coppery color with a darker back. In some regions the breast is grayish instead of copper.

Natural History: Rails are a fun and interesting family of birds. Shy and secretive, they skulk along at the edge of aquatic vegetation, wading in the sediment on large feet, poking in the shallows for food and darting in and out of cover. If disturbed even slightly, the rail quickly fades out of sight amidst the vegetation. Even one in plain sight may be impossible to spot because its camouflaging plumage disguises it so well against the vegetation. So shy is the rail that if you see it, you can be sure the rail doesn't see you. Catching sight of a rail is like being privy to a secret.

California's clapper rail is a special bird even in this special family. Three subspecies inhabit our state—the California clapper rail of central California is found mainly around San Francisco and San Pablo Bays; the light-footed clapper rail inhabits southern coastal marshes from Santa Barbara to San Diego; the Yuma clapper rail favors freshwater desert habitats along the lower Colorado River. Clapper rails are quite dependent upon their particular habitats, the coastal subspecies needing cordgrass and pickleweed marshes. Draining of coastal marshes has greatly affected populations of this secretive bird, making clapper rails both a California and federal endangered species. The entire U.S. population may number less than 2,000 birds. The rails' secretive habits don't help their recovery; very little is known about the birds' habits and life history because rails aren't easy to study.

Even if you don't see a clapper rail, you may hear its loud, carrying call, a repetitive *kik-kik-kik* sounding across the salt marsh. These clattering cackles reminded early settlers of old-fashioned clappers, hence the name clapper rail.

When and Where to See Them: Year-round in central and southern California, in tidal marshes of cordgrass and pickleweed and in freshwater marshes of southeastern deserts.

Clapper Rail (light-footed form)

BLACK-BELLIED PLOVER
Pluvialis squatarola
Family: Plovers
A.K.A.: bullhead, whistling plover, gray plover

Eye-catchers: To recognize a black-belly among other wintering shorebirds, look for its stocky build, short thick bill, faint white eyebrow, white rump and tail, and black "armpits" visible in flight.

In winter plumage this large plover is a nondescript gray, darker on the back and lighter underneath, with a faint pale eyebrow, sturdy bill, and black "armpits." In spring the male dons his breeding plumage—his face, throat, and belly turn coal black and his back and wings are patterned in black and white.

Natural History: California's mild winter attracts not only sunshine-seeking tourists but also migratory birds seeking a winter haven. Like those tourists, many of the birds have put away their best breeding plumage and are wearing winter casual, another word for drab. Despite its name, you will look in vain for this plover's black belly in winter. While the breeding black-bellied plover is flashily dressed in a coat of black and white, his face, throat, and underside painted a dramatic black, the wintering plover looks like a big gray sandpiper with a few speckles on its back.

The black-bellied plover is the largest of the short-billed sandpipers known as plovers and one of the most numerous of California shorebirds. It spends winter days patrolling sandy beaches and tidal flats seeking tiny shellfish, insects, marine worms, and other invertebrate animals that make up its diet. Not ones to overlook an opportunity, plovers may show up in newly plowed fields near the coast, eating the worms and grasshoppers turned up by plowing, and also eating seeds. The black-bellied plover is a wary bird, often the first among a group of foraging shorebirds to take flight at the hint of danger. The plover scurries along keeping a watchful eye, grabs a bit of food, then scurries further.

In April black-bellied plovers leave California for the long trip to their northern nesting grounds on the Arctic tundra of Canada and Alaska. Before they leave we may finally have the chance to see them outfitted for breeding, black bellies and all.

In winter California beaches also host the **semipalmated plover,** which looks like a small killdeer but with only one black neck ring, and the **snowy plover,** a small, pale plover with white undersides and black bars on the shoulders rather than a neck ring.

When and Where to See Them: From October to early April on tidal flats, estuaries, beaches, and breakwaters the length of the California coast.

Black-bellied Plover in winter plumage

Black-bellied Plover male in breeding plumage

*Semipalmated Plover male
in breeding plumage*

Snowy Plover male in breeding plumage

BLACK OYSTERCATCHER

Haematopus bachmani
Family: Oystercatchers
A.K.A.: redbill

Eye-catchers: The oystercatcher's specialized red bill, twice as long as the bird's head and flattened laterally, stands in sharp contrast to its black plumage. Its pale yellow eye is also distinctive.

This all-black bird has a distinctive bright red bill, pale eyes, and pink legs and feet.

Natural History: Many birds have tools adapted to their particular lifestyle, and the bill of the oystercatcher is among the finest examples. Compressed on the sides, the oystercatcher's bill is shaped a bit like the double-edged knives oystermen use to open and scrape the shells of their catch. The top of the bill is formed like a chisel; with it the bird pries shells off of rocks and pokes into the half-opened shells of its prey. Once that sharp bill is inside the shell, it severs the abductor muscle that holds the bivalve shell closed, and the bird dines on the exposed flesh within. Oysters are not the only items on the oystercatcher's menu. It feeds also on mussels, chitons, barnacles, clams, and limpets and pokes around in the mud and sand for crabs, marine worms, and other small animals.

Unlike most birds, oystercatchers have only three toes on each foot, not four, with all three toes pointing forward. Oystercatchers are often seen on rocky ledges and exposed rock breakers, where they search for food as the outgoing tide exposes shellfish on the rocks. The black bird with its flashy red bill makes a distinctive sight, plodding along with determination, turning with jerky movements this way and that as it searches for prey.

Oystercatchers do not leave California to nest but stay here year-round. Come spring the female oystercatcher makes a small hollow in the beach sand or among the rocks, safe above the tide line, where she lays her eggs. Both parents incubate the eggs and care for the hatchlings, which within about three days of hatching are running around the beach with their parents. In winter oystercatchers stay in the same neighborhood where they nested, sometimes gathering into small flocks.

When and Where to See Them: On rocky shores, reefs, breakwaters, and offshore islands year-round along California's coasts.

Black Oystercatcher

BLACK-NECKED STILT

Himantopus mexicanus
Family: Stilts and avocets
A.K.A.: daddy longlegs, longshanks, lawyerbird

Eye-catchers: There is no mistaking the stilt's slim-legged form, its needle-like bill, and its formal black-and-white plumage.

This slim, long-legged wader is handsomely patterned in large blocks of black and white, with a long, straight black bill, pink or red legs, and red eyes.

Natural History: If ever a bird was well-named, it is the stilt. It stands on impossibly long, twiglike legs that don't look like they could support a feather, much less an entire bird. The stilt's bill is likewise extremely long, slender, and needle-like, curving upward ever so slightly as if reflecting a sense of personal hauteur. In flight the stilt carries its legs trailing out behind like streamers. Despite its elegant appearance, once disturbed, the stilt becomes a shrill, screaming harpie, taking flight and circling with much loud and persistent calling— *keek, keek, keek.* This incessant, persistent racket led to the stilt being nicknamed "lawyer bird."

Stilts nest on the ground in loose colonies with others of their kind. They practice an interesting method of keeping themselves and their eggs cool. Sitting in the hot sun all day might kill the black-plumaged female and allow her eggs to overheat, so she makes as many as 100 trips a day to the water for a dip to soak her belly feathers. Once back atop her nest, the evaporation of the water keeps the adult and the eggs cool.

In fall stilts sometimes gather on tidal flats in flocks numbering in the thousands, presenting a milling mass that turns the sand to a checkerboard of black and white. They often feed in company with their long-legged cousin the American avocet.

When and Where to See Them: Year-round from San Francisco Bay south and at the Salton Sea, in summer in northern California and the Central Valley, and in spring and fall in southwestern valleys and deserts on shallow sloughs, tidal flats, fresh- and saltwater ponds, and flooded fields.

Black-necked Stilt male

AMERICAN AVOCET

Recurvirostra americana
Family: Stilts and avocets
A.K.A.: bluestocking, Irish snipe, yelper

Eye-catchers: With its unique upcurved bill, long legs, and bold rust, black, and white coloration, the avocet stands out in any crowd.

This stilt-legged wader's body is distinctively patterned in black and white. The neck and head are rusty orange and the long, needle-like bill curves gracefully upward. In winter the rusty head and neck fade to dull gray.

Natural History: An elegant bird moves gracefully in the shallows, stepping regally on pencil-thin legs as it bends to dabble in the water with its long bill. Despite a form that resembles cartoon character Olive Oyl—a full body set on impossibly-thin legs, long neck topped by a too-small head, and a knitting-needle bill that curves up ridiculously—the avocet is among the most beautiful and graceful of birds. Somehow its flowing lines and graceful moves transcend its seemingly mismatched parts. But the air of cool beauty dissolves once an intruder passes too close to an avocet's nest. Then the graceful bird transforms to virago, taking flight to dive-bomb the trespasser, screaming insistently with shrill cries that gather neighboring avocets in a communal mobbing of the threatening creature.

Look closely at a group of avocets and some may appear as if they've caught their bills in a door. The bill of the female curves up at a bit more of an angle than the male's longer and straighter bill. Bird bills come in all shapes and sizes—short and thick for cracking seeds, long and heavy for pecking wood, sharp and curved for catching prey—so why does an avocet's bill curve up? This wader uses its own technique for gathering food, and its bill is an essential tool. Wading into the shallows, the avocet slips the curved part of its bill, which is vertically flattened, under the water. Sweeping its bill back and forth through the water to stir up the silt and surface slime, the bird dabbles up snails, insects, and other small animals. Often a group of avocets will form a feeding skirmish line, marching shoulder to shoulder through the water, the activities of each dislodging food that may be snapped up by its neighbor.

When and Where to See Them: Year-round on coastal mudflats, estuaries, ponds, and lagoons along all but the most northern coastlines, and on shallow ponds and sloughs of the Central Valley. In summer on northern inland lakes and in winter on the Salton Sea.

American Avocet female in breeding plumage

American Avocet male in winter plumage

WILLET

Catoptrophorus semipalmatus
Family: Sandpipers
A.K.A.: pill-willet, white-winged curlew, humility

Eye-catchers: The gray willet is a Ho-Hum Charlie until it takes flight; then its wings flash a startling black and white.

This large, gray sandpiper, lighter on its undersides, has a medium-length bill and shows black and bright white on its wings when it flies.

Natural History: The willet is living proof that you can't tell a book by its cover. Feeding along California beaches and coastlines, the willet is a nondescript gray, but startled into flight it suddenly turns into one of the most identifiable of shorebirds. When the willet unfolds its wide wings, it unfurls a set of semaphore flags that boldly flash black-white, black-white. The bird's bright white tail adds to the startling transformation, as does its shrill voice screaming *pill-will-willet!* Willets are among a group of noisy shorebirds nicknamed "tattlers" for their telltale screams that announce the presence of intruders.

Willets are mainly a winter visitor to California, though some nonbreeding birds remain year-round. Most willets depart in April for nesting grounds in the Northwest and Canada, on dunes and coastal islands as well as open prairies and mountain meadows. On their nesting grounds, the male willets put their dramatic wing colors to good use, flying above their territory flashing their wings to signal their mates and warn off competing males. If a bird of prey flies over the semicolonial nesting grounds, several male willets may band together to mob it, flying close and flashing their colors to distract the predator. If an intruder passes too close to the nest, the female may feign injury like a killdeer, the entire broken-wing act aided by the attention-grabbing colors of her wings.

Though we might think it odd to sit down to a dinner of shorebird, in the late 19th and early 20th centuries willets were hunted almost to extinction on the East Coast by market gunners. Today they have made a comeback in the Northeast, and western populations are strong.

When and Where to See Them: Late June to early May along the coast on beaches, tidal flats, salt marshes, breakwaters, and wet meadows the length of the state. In summer on inland lakes with adjacent wet meadows.

Willet

Willet in flight

WHIMBREL
Numenius phaeopus
Family: Sandpipers
A.K.A.: bluelegs, crooked-bill marlin, foolish curlew

Eye-catchers: Look for the whimbrel's striped head, large size, and long down-curving bill.

This large, mottled brown shorebird has a long down-curved bill, dark stripes across the crown of the head, a dark streak through the eye, and blue gray legs.

Natural History: You gotta love a bird named "whimbrel." Found throughout the Northern Hemisphere, the bird gained its name in England, where coastal folk described its whistling *whi whi whi whi* call as "whim," adding "brel" as a diminutive. Thus, the whimbrel is "the little one that cries *whim*." The whimbrel is a curlew, one of a group of large sandpipers with long, down-curved bills. Its wild and wary nature helped the whimbrel escape the fate of the Eskimo curlew, which was slaughtered by hunters in the 19th century. The whimbrel stands in the shadow of its cousin the long-billed curlew, being smaller and having a shorter bill. Even so, the whimbrel is a delight to watch, and is easily identified by its head stripes. Because a whimbrel needs a large foraging area to find sufficient food, it usually stands as the only one of its kind amid a group of dowitchers, willets, and other shorebirds. If you look closely at these mixed flocks you will notice each species has a different bill length. The different birds can feed together without competing for food because they each probe at a different level in the sand—the whimbrel's long bill pokes in the farthest, then the dowitcher's, then the relatively short bill of the willet. Deep in the sand the whimbrel finds the marine worms, mollusks, crustaceans, and other animals that make up its diet.

Whimbrels pass through California during migration, following the coast as they move north in spring to their tundra nesting grounds at the edge of the Arctic Circle in far-northern Canada and Alaska, then showing up again on southward migration to wintering grounds in Central and South America. A flock of 10,000 whimbrels was sighted at the Salton Sea in spring of 1970. Some whimbrels remain in California throughout winter along the central and southern coasts.

When and Where to See Them: Mid-March to mid-May and late June to late September on coastal beaches, tidal flats, estuaries, breakwaters, and flooded fields the length of the state.

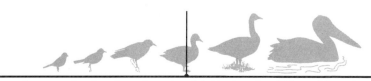

Whimbrel

LONG-BILLED CURLEW

Numenius americanus
Family: Sandpipers
A.K.A.: sabrebill, big curlew, smoker

Eye-catchers: The curlew's elongated bill, which is more than half the length of its body, identifies it anywhere.

This very large sandpiper is a mottled brown with cinnamon underparts and a very, very long, down-curved bill.

Natural History: From a human perspective, the long-billed curlew looks like nothing so much as a joke of nature. How, we might wonder, could any bird possibly have such an incredibly long bill? How does it keep from accidentally stubbing it in the sand and tumbling end over end? If one of us had a nose like that, we couldn't reach a doorknob, go through a revolving door, or look at ourself in a mirror without binoculars!

All references to Cyrano de Bergerac and Pinocchio aside, the curlew's bill is actually an extreme of physical adaptation. Shorebirds use their bills to probe in the sand and mud for food. The longer the bill, the deeper a bird can probe. With the longest bill of all, the curlew takes advantage of a feeding level beyond the reach of other probing shorebirds, thus exploiting an available ecological niche without any competition. You might think of curlews as the giraffes of the shorebird world.

The long-billed curlew sounds the lonesome call of its kind, a mournful *cur-lee!* that rises on the second syllable as if querying an unseen companion. In flight the curlew cuts a breathtaking figure. Its stretched-out body, long legs trailing, is led by the magnificent long bill. A curlew in flight cannot be mistaken for any other bird. Oddly enough, these shorebirds once nested throughout the great central prairies of the U.S., but plowing and development of native grasslands, as well as excessive hunting on the East Coast, have made curlews a rare sight in much of their former range.

Long-billed curlews are mainly a winter visitor in California, though some stay to breed in the state.

When and Where to See Them: Late June through April on tidal flats, salt marshes, estuaries, and wet meadows and fields the length of the state.

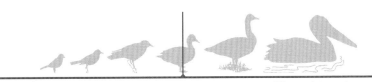

Long-billed Curlew

MARBLED GODWIT

Limosa fedoa
Family: Sandpipers
A.K.A.: spikebill, badger bird, red curlew

Eye-catchers: The godwit's long, two-toned bill—pink with a dusky tip—identifies it among similar shorebirds.

The back of this large brown shorebird is mottled with black and cinnamon. Its long bill, which curves up very slightly, is distinctively colored pink with a dark tip.

Natural History: Like so many of the shorebirds, the marbled godwit is named for its haunting call—*god WIT, god WIT, god WIT.* The "marbled" part of its name comes from the pattern of its plumage. Powerful fliers, godwits migrate in long, trailing lines, the tips of which seem to waver as leaders switch off with other birds. The marbled godwit shares with the long-billed curlew not only large size (it is smaller than the curlew) and long bill but a tragic recent history. Godwits were slaughtered along the East Coast by hunters in the 19th century, although they once migrated in great flocks, they are now a rare sight in the East. Like the long-billed curlew, the marbled godwit nests on interior prairies, preferring the prairie pothole regions of Canada and the northern states, and it, too, has seen its nesting habitat lost to agriculture and development.

The marbled godwit wades on its long legs thigh-deep into the water, where it thrusts its head beneath the surface and probes in the sand for shellfish, snails, marine worms, and other small animals. With the nerve-rich, sensitive tip of its bill it can feel for its food, a good idea since its quarry is buried in the sand underwater and a trombone's length from its eyes. Like the other long-billed waders, the godwit is often seen in mixed flocks with other species whose varying bill lengths allow all to feed over the same ground but at different depths, without competing with each other.

In spring the flashy aerial courtship displays of the godwit can be quite a sight as it carves figure eights in the air, its screaming *ratica-ratica-ratica* calls making it a hard bird to ignore.

When and Where to See Them: Mid-July through May in salt marshes, wet meadows, estuaries, tidal flats, and beaches the length of the state.

Marbled Godwit

BLACK TURNSTONE

Arenaria melanocephala
Family: Sandpipers
A.K.A.: rock plover

Eye-catchers: In its busy foraging habits the turnstone is true to its name.

The turnstone is dusky black with a white belly, dark legs, and a short, slightly upturned bill. In breeding plumage it gains a round white spot in front of the eyes. In flight the turnstone's wings flash a bold pattern of black and white.

Natural History: From its name, it's not hard to figure out how this bird seeks food. The turnstone moves along the sea's edge, turning over stones, shells, dirt clods, and even clumps of seaweed seeking snails, mollusks, crabs, and any other small marine creatures that might make a meal.

The black turnstone is not a beach lover, inhabiting instead rocky coasts, barnacle-covered reefs, and offshore rocky islands and ledges. The turnstone is hard to spot due to its camouflaging plumage when it stands motionless, which, lucky for birdwatchers, isn't often. Turnstones are always marching around turning over and peeking under beach detritus like busybodies.

From its nesting grounds on coastal tundra in Alaska, the black turnstone shows up on California beaches to spend fall and winter, becoming a busy beachcomber. Once on wintering grounds, turnstones gather together in feeding flocks, the entire group keeping up a low-level chatter. If one bird is spooked and takes flight, its startling flash of black-and-white wings sends a warning to its fellows, who will also take flight, the entire group twinkling suddenly like a crowd in a football stadium signaling with two-toned placards.

When and Where to See Them: Mid-July to late April on rocky coasts and beaches the length of the state.

Black Turnstone in winter

SANDERLING

Calidris alba
Family: Sandpipers
A.K.A.: beach bird, surf snipe, bull peep

Eye-catchers: The plump sanderling's busy beach scurrying, moving up and back with the waves, makes it the most familiar of shorebirds.

These plump little sandpipers are very pale in winter plumage—pale gray on the back and white on the undersides with a short neck, small head, and fairly short, straight bill. In breeding plumage the head, breast, and back are mottled a darker gray and white with a reddish wash.

Natural History: As ubiquitous as the waves, the sanderling is perhaps the most familiar and endearing bird of the California beaches. Moving just at the dry edge of each breaking wave, ever busy, ever moving flocks of sanderlings scurry along the beach, investigating the treasures brought ashore by each pulse of the ocean. Like a group of kids afraid to get their feet wet, sanderlings move out onto the wet sand as each wave recedes, scurrying just out of the way of the water as the next wave comes in and offering endless amusement to beachgoers. Their short black legs seem to move impossibly fast, scuttling the plump gray birds back and forth on the beach.

While many small sandpipers feed in big flocks, a group of sanderlings spreads out in a line, breaking into smaller groups of a few birds like soccer teams spread out across the tide line. They are quite tolerant of humans, sometimes allowing observers to draw within 2 to 3 feet. Unfortunately this also means they are often chased by children and dogs, which can interfere with their feeding. Sanderlings will follow along after turnstones, picking over the patches of beach exposed by the other birds' activity.

The smallest of North American sandpipers, the **least sandpiper,** is also a common winter coastal visitor. Its brownish plumage, yellowish green legs, and tiny size help identify it.

When and Where to See Them: From July to late May along beaches and sea-coasts the length of the state.

Sanderlings

Least Sandpiper juvenile

SHORT-BILLED DOWITCHER

Limnodromus griseus
Family: Sandpipers
A.K.A.: brown back, robin snipe, sea pigeon

Eye-catchers: The dowitcher's plump body led by a very long bill help identify it. Its call is a low *tu tu tu.*

In winter the dowitcher has a gray brown back and lighter undersides. In summer its underparts become cinnamon red. This medium-size sandpiper has a chunky body, relatively short legs, and a very long bill. In flight watch for the barred tail and white rump.

Natural History: While the godwit, curlew, and whimbrel are long-legged, big birds with really long bills, the short-billed dowitcher and its cousin, the **long-billed dowitcher,** are short-legged, medium-size birds with really long bills. Because of their stature, dowitchers lack the elegant appearance of the larger birds and look more awkward and chubby. The two dowitcher species look very much alike, and since they often feed together in flocks, they can create a headache for those concerned with exactly identifying one versus the other. You would think bill length would be the key, but that is not always reliable. The best way to tell the two apart is by their calls. The long-billed gives one or more high-pitched *keek* notes, while the short-billed calls with a softer *tu tu tu.* Long-bills also prefer freshwater habitats in winter and migration, while short-bills favor tidal flats.

Dowitchers are fun shorebirds to watch, comical with their tubby bodies, short legs, and absurdly long bills. With its bill the dowitcher busily probes the sand in a rapid up-and-down sewing-machine motion, a feeding action similar to that of its freshwater cousins the snipe and the woodcock. Dowitchers are social birds and may gather in flocks not just with long-billed dowitchers but with godwits, willets, and other waders, the mixed group feeding at different levels in the sand or mud, depending on bill length. At the approach of danger, dowitchers take to the air in wheeling, fast-flying groups, twisting and turning as they call loudly.

When and Where to See Them: From early July to mid-May along the coast the length of the state in estuaries, tidal flats, salt marshes, and lagoons, as well as freshwater marshes and pond edges during migration.

Short-billed Dowitchers

Long-billed Dowitcher in winter

WILSON'S PHALAROPE

Phalaropus tricolor
Family: Sandpipers
A.K.A.: summer phalarope

Eye-catchers: The breeding Wilson's phalarope is distinctive for its dark gray, white, and cinnamon head and neck, but it is the phalarope's behavior on the water, pirouetting left and right as it swims, that truly identifies it.

In summer the phalarope has pale undersides, a gray brown back, a cinnamon wash on the neck, and a broad dark streak that passes through the eye and down the side of the neck. In winter plumage it is gray above with white underparts. Phalaropes have a small head, long thin neck, and long straight bill.

Natural History: Nature seems to have created endless versions of waterbirds, and phalaropes have unique traits of their own. When you first witness the behavior of phalaropes feeding on the water you may think you've stumbled upon a band of whirling dervishes. Phalaropes paddle about jerkily on shallow water, making sudden turns left or right and stabbing repeatedly with their bills. They often spin on the water, sometimes making 60 revolutions a minute, looking like avian tops gone wild. But there is method to their madness. As they whirl they stir up the bottom, dislodging insects, larvae, brine shrimp, and other food, which the birds promptly gobble up.

Phalaropes exhibit another remarkable trait. Unlike most bird species, it is the prerogative of the female phalarope to court the male. The female is also larger and more colorful. When a male catches her fancy, she follows him around on the water, lowering her head and flying at any other females who come near. Once she is ready to mate, the male lifts off, then hovers over her like a helicopter before landing on her back for the actual mating. He also usually builds the nest and is left with child care duties when the female departs after laying the eggs. The male even develops brood patches—bare spots—on his abdomen, which become engorged with blood and help keep the eggs and young warm.

Though on the east side of the Sierra Nevada and far from the ocean, Mono Lake is a wonderful place to witness an astounding gathering of Wilson's phalaropes in July. As many as 90,000 of the birds have been counted there as they gather to migrate, feasting on the millions of brine flies and brine shrimp found in the lake.

When and Where to See Them: Mid-April to mid-May and mid-June to September on coastal lagoons, bays, estuaries, and ponds, also flooded fields and marshy edges of ponds and lakes. From June to early August thousands gather on Mono Lake.

Wilson's Phalarope juvenile

HEERMANN'S GULL

Larus heermanni
Family: Gulls and terns
A.K.A.: white-headed gull

Eye-catchers: This gull's bloodred bill, pearl gray body, black tail, and white head, turning streaky in winter, help identify it.

In summer this dark gray gull has a black tail, white head, and bright red bill. In winter the head becomes streaked with gray.

Natural History: Identifying gulls can be a nightmare for birdwatchers, but luckily the Heermann's gull is among the easiest to pin down due to its dark gray body, red bill, and white head, which gets streaky in winter. Though these gulls take three years to reach their adult plumage, the chocolate brown young birds stand out from other gulls.

Heermann's gulls nest on islands off the west coast of Mexico, heading north along the California coast in midsummer after the breeding season, an upside-down version of the migration pattern of most North American birds, which move south after the breeding season.

Gulls could never be accused of being quiet birds, and the Heermann's is no exception. Its call is a whining, catlike mew—*whee-ee*—and when high overhead it often cries out over and over, *cow-auk! cow-eek!* Heermann's gulls hunt offshore for fish, crustaceans, and mollusks and join other gulls to scavenge along beaches. Gulls are supreme marauders and opportunists, and Heermann's gulls will harass brown pelicans and cormorants, attempting to snatch fish from the mouths of the larger birds. They have also learned to drop shellfish onto rocks to crack open the shells.

The **western gull** is a year-round denizen of California seashores. In mature plumage it has a classic gull appearance—white body with dark back and wings and pink feet. Watch for them following boats in hopes of a handout.

When and Where to See Them: Along seacoasts, estuaries, harbors, and offshore islands the length of the state, particularly the central and southern coasts, throughout the year.

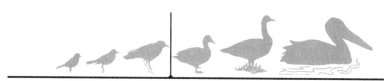

Heermann's Gull in breeding plumage

Heermann's Gull juvenile

Western Gull in winter plumage

FORSTER'S TERN

Sterna forsteri
Family: Gulls and terns
A.K.A.: marsh tern, sea swallow

Eye-catchers: The jaunty black cap of the summer Forster's tern, fading to a black patch around the eye in winter, identifies it, as does its pale body.

This white tern has a pale gray mantle, deeply forked tail, and orange bill with black tip. In summer a black cap comes down to the eye line, but it fades to white in winter except for a black patch around the eye.

Natural History: A sleek, slim white bird flies above a calm lagoon, its pointed head angled down as it scans the water. Though gull-like in appearance, it is smaller and more slender than a gull, its wings tapered and pointed and its tail beautifully forked like that of a barn swallow. Suddenly it pauses, hovering over the water like an avian helicopter, then plunges into the water bill-first to grab a meal.

Compared to the raucous, marauding behavior of the stout-bodied gull, the swift, dramatic fishing style and sleek, trim body of the tern is like the difference between a rugby player and a gymnast. First cousins to gulls, terns are smaller, more slender, and more graceful, with tapered, pointed wings and deeply forked tails, leading to a common nickname, "sea swallow." While gulls land on the water or shore to feed, bobbing easily on the waves or foraging on beaches and rocks, terns typically plunge-dive from the air into the water after prey. Terns are buoyant but their webbed feet are too small and weak to effectively paddle, thus they do not land on water as often as gulls.

The **least tern,** smallest of North American terns, breeds in summer along the California coast between San Francisco Bay and San Diego. Least terns are listed both federally and in California as an endangered species. In the 19th century they were slaughtered by the hundreds of thousands for the millinery trade, their wings and entire skins being used to decorate women's hats.

When and Where to See Them: Year-round on seacoasts, lagoons, harbors, and estuaries, particularly along the central and southern coasts. At the Salton Sea mid-April to mid-September.

Forster's Tern in breeding plumage

Forster's Tern in first-winter plumage

Least Tern with young

BLACK SKIMMER

Rhynchops niger
Family: Skimmers
A.K.A.: knifebill, cut-water, sea dog

Eye-catchers: Flying just above the water surface, its lower bill skimming the water, the skimmer is like no other North American bird.

The skimmer looks as if someone dipped it in black ink up to its midline, being black above from head to tail and white below. The red bill is black-tipped, with the lower mandible longer than the upper.

Natural History: Without warning, a fast-flying, scimitar-winged group of black-and-white birds materializes above the still waters of a salt pond in south San Diego Bay, working back and forth across it like hunting dogs quartering a field by scent. But instead of flying well above the water like terns or ospreys, the birds fly fast and low just above the water, trailing the lower mandibles of their bills in the water.

If ever a creature was wonderfully adapted to a very specific mode of life it is the black skimmer. While other waterbirds dive after fish from the surface, plunge-dive from the air, poke in the sand, or dabble in the sediment, the skimmer hunts the top few inches of the water, using speed and specialized technique to catch prey. Unique in the bird world, the skimmer's lower mandible is longer than the upper, and compressed laterally into a knife-edge that cuts the water. The lower bill grows faster than the upper to accommodate for the friction and wear of the water. When the bill touches a fish, the upper bill snaps down. Avoiding detection by its prey is important, and the skimmer's counter-shaded plumage—black above the midline and white below—camouflages it from fish looking up from below. The white underside makes the bird almost invisible against the sky, the black dorsal surface erasing any shapes and shadows.

Black skimmers began showing up in southern California in the early 1960s, expanding their range north from Mexico. Nesting was first confirmed, at the Salton Sea, in 1972. Now skimmers are well-established in south San Diego Bay, Bolsa Chica State Ecological Reserve, and the Salton Sea, and they show up increasingly in other areas of southern and central California.

When and Where to See Them: Year-round on quiet, shallow, saltwater lagoons and ponds of south San Diego Bay and Bolsa Chica State Ecological Reserve. April to mid-October on the Salton Sea.

Black Skimmer

Salton Sea

Lower Klamath National Wildlife Refuge

BIRDS OF FRESHWATER
Rivers, Lakes, Marshes, and Streamside Woodlands

Pied-billed Grebe
American White Pelican
Double-crested Cormorant
Great Blue Heron
Great Egret
Snowy Egret/Cattle Egret
Black-crowned Night-Heron
White-faced Ibis
Tundra Swan
Snow Goose/
   Greater White-fronted Goose/
   Ross's Goose/Canada Goose
Green-winged Teal/
   Cinnamon Teal
Mallard
Northern Shoveler
Ruddy Duck
Bald Eagle
American Coot
Sandhill Crane
Killdeer
Spotted Sandpiper

Common Snipe
Ring-billed Gull/California Gull
Great Horned Owl
Belted Kingfisher
Black Phoebe
Barn Swallow
Yellow-billed Magpie
Marsh Wren/House Wren
Ruby-crowned Kinglet
Cedar Waxwing
Yellow Warbler/
   Common Yellowthroat
Yellow-rumped Warbler
Lazuli Bunting
Song Sparrow
Red-winged Blackbird/
   Yellow-headed Blackbird
Brewer's Blackbird/
   Brown-headed Cowbird
Bullock's Oriole
American Goldfinch/
   Lesser Goldfinch

PIED-BILLED GREBE

Podilymbus podiceps
Family: Grebes
A.K.A.: dabchick, hell diver, water witch

Eye-catchers: Watch for this grebe's rounded body, short bill, and habit of suddenly disappearing underwater only to bob up somewhere else.

A small, short-tailed, ducklike bird with a rounded head and snubbed dark and white bill.

Natural History: *Pied* is an archaic word meaning "black and white," and with this small waterbird it refers to the dark ring present around the adult's white bill during breeding season. Though pied-billed grebes are among the most common of waterbirds and are found throughout North America, they are always a delight to see. On a busy pond, among the larger ducks and geese, pied-billed grebes look like little bobbing dinghies. This grebe came by two of its nicknames—"water witch" and "hell diver"—because of its disappearing act. One moment the grebe floats unconcerned on the water; the next moment it suddenly arches its neck and dives nose-first into the water. In a few moments the grebe bobs up again as if nothing has happened. Sometimes the pied-billed grebe does a submarine impression; if startled, it slowly sinks below the water until only the top of its head remains, like a periscope.

Grebes are often mistaken for ducks, but they actually are a family unto themselves. Where ducks have webbed feet, grebes have flaps of skin called lobes protruding from their toes. Grebes also have a pointed, chickenlike bill instead of the spatulate bill of a duck. They build floating nests of reeds and the leaves of pond vegetation. Once the young hatch, they ride on their parents' backs, holding on to the adult's feathers with their bills and going along for the ride when the parent dives.

When and Where to See Them: Throughout the state on freshwater ponds and marshes year-round.

Pied-billed Grebe in breeding plumage

AMERICAN WHITE PELICAN

Pelecanus erythrorhynchos
Family: Pelicans
A.K.A.: white pelican

Eye-catchers: In flight, pelicans seem almost like small aircraft, and on the ground they look like white sailing ships.

This big white bird with black wingtips has a long, curving neck and long, orange bill equipped with a skin pouch. Except in flight or while fishing, the bill is held close to the body. In flight white pelicans can be distinguished from snow geese and whooping cranes by their body shape and large size.

Natural History: With its dumpy body, short legs, and ridiculous bill, the pelican seems like a cartoon character. But the white pelican is marvelously designed for its lifestyle. Unlike brown pelicans, which dive into deep water from the air, white pelicans float on the surface of shallow water and scoop fish up in their dipnet-style bills. The bird's flexible lower jaw flares out like a hoop, stretching the skin pouch, which can hold several gallons of water. Once filled, the lower bill is squeezed to push out the water and any fish are gulped down.

Most remarkable is the white pelican's technique of cooperative fishing. A group of pelicans works together in a skirmish line, splashing and paddling, to drive fish into shallow water, where they are then gobbled up. Sometimes two lines of pelicans will swim toward each other, trapping fish in a pincer movement. A group of fishing pelicans often paddles along, rhythmically dipping their bills in slow unison like a rowing crew—dip together, dip; dip together, dip. Even in flight pelicans demonstrate a military precision, as they circle and bank in perfect unison or wing along at high altitudes in a carefully spaced line. The white pelican's 9-foot wingspan is the largest of any bird in North America with the exception of the California condor.

In late winter, adult pelicans develop a bump on the top of their bill that serves to attract pelicans of the opposite sex and signals readiness to mate. Pelicans nest in summer on protected islands in the middle of lakes or other bodies of water. They may fly as much as 50 miles one way in order to find food. The birds then return to the nest and regurgitate the food for their young.

When and Where to See Them: Statewide in migration, primarily from March to May, and again in October, on shallow bodies of freshwater as well as bays, estuaries, and other shallow marine environs. In winter on coastal bays and lagoons and inland on lakes from the Central Valley south. Upwards of 10,000 winter on the Salton Sea.

American White Pelican

American White Pelicans feeding

DOUBLE-CRESTED CORMORANT

Phalacrocorax auritus
Family: Cormorants
A.K.A.: shag, taunton turkey

Eye-catchers: The perched cormorant is unmistakable with its curving neck and upright posture, often perched with its wings held out.

A large, black waterbird with a hooked bill and a patch of bare yellow skin under the bill. Breeding adults have two feathery "crests" on the head.

Natural History: The double-crested cormorant is the only California cormorant species found regularly on freshwater, and thus the only one regularly seen inland. Since it is more widespread, it is also the cormorant watchers are most likely to encounter.

Cormorants ride low in the water, with neck curved snakelike and head tipped slightly up, "nose in the air." They are superb fishers, diving underwater and chasing down their prey. A cormorant's legs are attached at the very end of its body, rather than underneath like a duck's. Using their feet as paddles to propel themselves forward they flap their wings to "fly" underwater. Their hooked bills help them hang on to slippery fish. They may dive as deep as 25 feet, staying underwater up to 70 seconds.

Rocks and logs around lakes are good places to spot resting cormorants as they sit in the sun with their wings spread-eagled to dry. Though cormorants are waterbirds, their feathers are designed to reduce buoyancy and help them dive and pursue fish underwater. The downside of this means their feathers don't repel water very well, and after a swim the cormorant must dry its wings in the sun. Luckily the cormorant has a waterproof inner layer of feathers near the body, so its coat may get wet but inside it stays dry and warm.

Cormorants are sociable birds, building basket-shaped nests of sticks in the upper branches of trees and shrubs around lakes and reservoirs. Because of their size and long necks cormorants often look like geese when in flight. But while geese honk noisily, cormorants are more discreet and maintain their silence. Their "flap, flap, cruise" flying pattern also differs from the goose's steady wing beats.

When and Where to See Them: Year-round, though more commonly August through May, on inland freshwater lakes, reservoirs, and large streams mainly in central and southern California, and large bays, salt ponds, and lagoons all along the coast. In summer, in nesting colonies on lakes in the mountains and northeastern plateau.

Double-crested Cormorant in breeding plumage

Double-crested Cormorant drying wings

MALLARD
Anas platyrhynchos
Family: Swans, geese, and ducks
A.K.A.: greenhead, curlytail

Eye-catchers: The familiar gleaming emerald head of the male mallard is its defining crown.

The male mallard is a large duck with an iridescent green head that appears dark blue or purple in some light. He has a yellow bill, white neck ring, chestnut breast, gray back, and curly tail. The female is a mottled brown.

Natural History: Have you ever passed by a pond and seen its surface covered with feathery duck rumps, all pointing toward the sky? Mallards are dabbling ducks, meaning they sit on the surface of shallow water and duck their heads under to reach aquatic plants, insects, and detritus in the mud, so it is a common sight to see them tipped "bottoms up."

If you can recognize no other duck in the wild, you ought to be able to recognize a mallard. This large duck with the hallmark green head is found throughout the Northern Hemisphere and is the ancestor of all breeds of domestic duck except the Muscovy. Indeed, mallards seem ready and willing to live closely with humans, taking up residence in parks, golf courses, even backyard ponds and swimming pools, and having no qualms about being hand-fed. The loud *QUACK, quack, quack* of the female mallard is the signature sound of ducks to most people.

To human eyes, the mallard pair makes a charming couple, swimming quietly side by side on the water, the male seeming attentive and solicitous of his mate. Then comes the actual mating act, which has startled many a naive viewer feeding ducks in the park. The male chases the female around, in and out of the water, finally climbing up on her back and pecking her head rather aggressively, pushing it underwater. Despite the surprise and shock of onlookers, the female is none the worse, shaking her head and paddling off once things are finished. Her mate departs once the eggs are laid. Soon after hatching the downy yellow-and-black ducklings follow their mother to water and swim dutifully behind her like a string of fluffy beads.

When and Where to See Them: Statewide year-round on freshwater lakes, ponds, rivers, and flooded fields, and in urban parks, ponds, and golf courses.

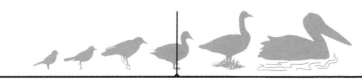

Great Blue Heron

GREAT EGRET

Ardea alba

Family: Herons

A.K.A.: American egret, angel bird, white crane, plume bird

Eye-catchers: The ghostly shape of this large, white bird, poised motionless at the edge of water or in a flooded farm field, can't be missed.

This tall wading bird is snowy white, with black legs and yellow bill. Its shape is slender, with the long neck, bill, and legs typical of herons.

Natural History: Posed like a white shadow at the water's edge, wading elegantly on sleek black legs, or winging past like an angel headed for heaven, the great egret is one bird that never ceases to elicit awe and admiration from bird lovers. Great egrets are one of the most widely distributed of herons, nesting in temperate and tropical areas around the world. Though in places they are as common as crows, their large size and striking white color make great egrets perennial crowd pleasers. In contrast to its elegant appearance, the great egret's voice is hoarse and raucous, conjuring images of an out-of-sorts beauty queen.

Once great egrets discover a rich food source, they gather in large groups, often dotting a marsh or flooded field like a collection of long-legged white clouds. Like their close cousins the herons, egrets feed on a diverse collection of aquatic animal life, including fish, frogs, snakes, crayfish, and insects. Great egrets can be distinguished from snowy and cattle egrets by their much larger size and the combination of black legs and yellow bill. Though quite tall, great egrets have a slender shape and are not as large as great blue herons.

As great egrets come into the mating season, both male and female develop a flowing cape of long plumes called a nuptial train. The feathers of the cape may be as much as 4.5 feet long. Unfortunately for the birds, these spectacular plumes caught the eye of more than just other egrets. At the end of the 19th century and beginning of the 20th, egrets were killed in huge numbers by plume hunters who sold their feathers to adorn ladies' hats. Egret feathers sold for as much as $32 an ounce. Only a growing public outcry, and a change in millinery fashion, saved the great egret from extinction.

When and Where to See Them: Statewide on fresh- and saltwater marshes, lagoons, bays, estuaries, and freshwater lakes, rivers, flooded fields, and irrigation canals. More common along coastal areas in fall and winter, with an inland shift in spring for nesting.

Great Egret

SNOWY EGRET

Egretta thula
Family: Herons
A.K.A.: lesser egret, little snowy, little white egret

Eye-catchers: Watch for the snowy egret's puffy white shape at the water's edge or in a flooded field.

A medium-size, slender, all-white heron with black bill and legs and yellow feet.

Natural History: The snowy egret looks much like a mini-version of the great egret. It is a marvelous snow white, hence the name, and it has a black bill and black legs. Now here's the fun part—the elegant snowy egret wears yellow sneakers. This is not to make a fashion statement, but to aid the bird in hunting. Watch a snowy egret closely when you see it feeding at water's edge. Instead of standing motionless, it marches along lifting and swirling each foot in the water as it goes. This stirs up frogs, fish, and other food on the bottom, which the egret promptly gobbles down. The bright yellow feet, biologists theorize, may startle prey into motion; wouldn't you jump out of the way if you saw a garish yellow thing coming at you out of the murky depths? Sometimes snowy egrets dart quickly here and there, another version of the startle-your-prey-into-showing-itself tactic.

Like great egrets, snowies develop beautiful breeding plumage. Snowy egrets were nearly lost to the world because their nuptial plumage was highly prized for women's hats at the end of the 19th century.

Another medium-size white heron, the **cattle egret,** is often mistaken for a snowy. The cattle egret is stockier and has an orange bill and legs. During breeding season it also has orange feathers on its crown and breast. True to their name, cattle egrets often follow stock animals, feeding on insects stirred up by the grazing animals.

When and Where to See Them: Statewide along rivers, lakes, and streams during nesting season and in coastal lagoons, estuaries, and marshes from late summer to spring.

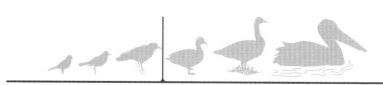

Snowy Egret

Cattle Egret colony

Cattle Egret in breeding plumage

BLACK-CROWNED NIGHT-HERON

Nycticorax nycticorax
Family: Herons
A.K.A.: quawk, plunket

Eye-catchers: Its slouched posture—head sunk between shoulders—and loud *Quok!* call identify the night-heron.

A medium-sized heron with a short neck and short legs, adults have a black back, gray wings and tail, white underside, red eyes, and black cap with long white plumes. Immatures are a streaky yellow and brown.

Natural History: While many of its heron cousins are blessed with the long, graceful limbs and neck of a model, the night-heron has the short-legged, no-neck appearance of a stolid peasant. Seeming to adopt the stereotypical sullen slouch of disaffected youth, the night-heron sits in a tree or on a rock at water's edge. But the night-heron is merely patient, not apathetic. It may stand without moving for long periods, waiting for small fish, its favorite prey, to swim within striking distance. Then zap, it grabs its prey, which includes frogs, crayfish, or even mice, with its razor bill and gobbles it down.

These small herons adapt well to life around humans, showing up at ponds in city parks as well as at busy harbors. They often build large nesting colonies in groves of trees, usually near water. As the young herons reach adult size and prepare to leave the nest, the colony becomes a noisy, active place as the youngsters stretch and test their wings, hop about the nest, and adults fly in and out with food.

The night-heron's Latin name, *nycticorax,* means night raven, a reference to its less-than-melodious call. Yet the loud, croaking *Quok!* that signals the bird's nightly feeding forays is a familiar and even endearing evening sound in many suburban and rural locales. Its flight profile is also distinctive—short-necked, with bill, back, and tail making one smooth line and the feet protruding just beyond the tail.

When and Where to See Them: Year-round in fresh- and saltwater marshes, estuaries, shores of lakes and rivers, and harbors and piers throughout the state except in mountain and desert regions. Common at the Salton Sea. Most active in morning and evening.

Black-crowned Night-Heron

Black-crowned Night-Heron juvenile

WHITE-FACED IBIS

Plegadis chihi
Family: Ibises
A.K.A.: black curlew

Eye-catchers: The down-curved bill of the ibis is unmistakable, whether the bird is in flight or on the ground.

A glossy bird that often appears black but in proper light is a rich bronze with green, copper, and red highlights. The ibis has long legs and neck and a long, down-curved bill. In breeding season, white feathers outline its face.

Natural History: It's no surprise that the curvilinear silhouette of the ibis conjures images of a creature both ancient and sacred. The white-faced ibis is cousin to the sacred ibis of Egypt, worshipped by ancient cultures and immortalized in hieroglyphics at least 5,000 years old. The ibis family is an ancient one; fossil evidence dates back 60 million years. The ibis's reptilian roots seem evident in its flying-dinosaur flight profile. Like their cousins the storks, ibises fly with legs held out behind and necks extended, displaying their distinctive curving bill. Their flight pattern is also distinguishing; groups of ibises fly in diagonal lines, or occasional Vs, alternately flapping and gliding in unison.

The ibis's genus name, *Plegadis,* means scythe, a reference to the bird's bill. This bill is a fine tool, an enormous, sensitive set of forceps with which the ibis probes in the mud and sand for crustaceans, snails, insects, worms, frogs, and other food. Prey is grabbed in the pincerlike grip of the bill, then swallowed as the bird suddenly tosses its head backward. A group of ibises will descend upon a mudflat and spread out in a skirmish line like a group of gleaners, busily probing and feeding.

Ibises are just as social during nesting season, when they nest in small colonies, sometimes with herons. Their nests, usually built among the tules and bulrushes, are deep cups woven from dead reeds and either float on rafts of plant material or are anchored to the reeds above the water.

When and Where to See Them: Throughout the state in farm fields, freshwater marshes, mudflats around lakes and ponds, and along irrigation canals. In northern California in summer and central and southern California fall through spring, with some birds visible year-round.

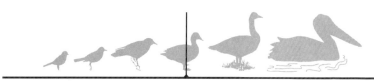

White-faced Ibis in winter plumage

TUNDRA SWAN
Cygnus columbianus
Family: Swans, geese, and ducks
A.K.A.: whistling swan, common swan

Eye-catchers: A large, white bird with a long, elegant neck and regal bearing can be nothing other than a swan.

A large, all-white waterbird with long neck, black bill, and a yellow spot near the eye.

Natural History: When Lewis and Clark explored the Far West in the early 19th century they saw on the Columbia River a bird new to them, a wild western cousin of the elegant white swans of Europe. Hearing the birds' soft, high-pitched musical calls, they named them whistling swans, which until recently was the accepted common name for the tundra swan. The sighting of this handsome species on the Columbia River is remembered in its species name, *columbianus.*

According to legend, the tundra swan gives a high, sweet call upon dying, known as a "swan song," described by noted ornithologist John K. Terres as "one of the most beautiful utterances of waterfowl—a melodious, soft, muted series of notes." Terres described this as a departure song, given before taking flight. Other versions describe the swan song less romantically, as the result of air escaping from the bird's long neck as it tumbles from the sky after being shot.

The tundra swan uses its long neck to advantage as it plunges its head below the water surface to feed on aquatic plants. Its probing and rooting in the silty mud aerates the sediment and encourages plant growth.

When you see a large, white waterbird, look closely. White pelicans, though larger than swans, have a very long orange bill. The snow goose, another long-necked, white waterfowl, is much smaller than a tundra swan, which may weigh as much as 18 pounds, and lacks the swan's characteristic elegant posture.

Tundra swans are winter birds in California, descending in fall upon the wetlands and refuges of the Central Valley and other areas, where they often crowd surrounding fields to feed on waste grain. Because the tundra swan calls during migration, you may be privy to its musical laughter while it is in California between fall and spring. When the swan departs California in spring, it begins a fantastic voyage to the Arctic tundra of Alaska, Canada, and Siberia, nesting literally at the top of the world.

When and Where to See Them: Mid-October to mid-March on large freshwater lakes and marshes and grainfields of the Central Valley.

Tundra Swans in flight

Tundra Swans

SNOW GOOSE

Chen caerulescens
Family: Swans, geese, and ducks
A.K.A.: blue goose (dark phase)

Eye-catchers: Trailing lines of angel white snow geese, their wing tips marked with black, fill the sky with their high-pitched honking.

This beautiful goose is dazzling white with black wing tips, pinkish legs, and black "lipstick" on the bill. The dark-phase "blue" goose is blue gray with a white head.

Natural History: The once-vast network of wetlands, marshes, and ponds in the valleys along the center of California is now vastly reduced, yet still offers vital wintering habitat for hundreds of thousands of geese and ducks. Though much of these natural wetlands have been drained for agriculture, numerous waterfowl refuges offer great opportunities for fall and winter waterfowl viewing.

The arrival and departure of waterfowl is never subtle. Standing at the edge of a marsh or lake as thousands of snow geese come in with a boisterous cacophony of honking and flapping is a wondrous sight. At dawn the birds rise up in groups and fill the sky as they move out to grainfields to feed. The evening fly-in is equally dramatic, as birds trail in from all points of the compass. At times the sky is so full of birds it seems that it couldn't possibly hold more, and the birds fly so close overhead the whoosh of their wings is audible and the powerful working of their flight muscles can be seen.

Snow geese fly in trailing lines or Us rather than the neat Vs of Canada geese. Their honking is different too, higher-pitched and not the classic *ho-onk*.

Snow geese are truly birds of the far north, nesting on the Arctic tundra of Canada, Alaska, and Siberia. Like many human snowbirds, they arrive in fall to spend the cold months in the relative warmth of California. Geese are grazers, feeding on grass, grains, and aquatic plants. A darker-colored form of the snow goose, the blue goose, was once considered an entirely different species until researchers observing a breeding colony near Hudson Bay noticed that the blue and white snow geese interbred and produced an intermediate, light gray morph of snow goose.

continued

Snow Goose in flight

Snow Geese at Sacramento National Wildlife Refuge

Snow Geese, with one in blue color phase

SNOW GOOSE

Chen caerulescens

Continued

Several other geese winter in California in large numbers. The **greater white-fronted goose** is a medium-size gray brown goose named somewhat oddly for the white band at the base of the bill. It is the earliest arriving of geese, showing up on northern California refuges beginning in late August. The **Ross's goose** is similar to the snow goose, though smaller. It is white with black wing tips, but has a shorter neck and a more rounded head and lacks the black "lipstick" of the snow goose. The Ross's also has a blue color phase that is extremely rare. The handsome **Canada goose** is a large, familiar, and abundant goose. It is gray brown with a black neck and head marked by a white chinstrap.

When and Where to See Them: From late September to mid-April on freshwater marshes and lakes and flooded farm fields, especially on waterfowl refuges, of the Klamath Basin, Sacramento, San Joaquin, Imperial, and lower Colorado River valleys.

*Greater White-
fronted Goose*

Ross's Goose

Canada Goose

GREEN-WINGED TEAL

Anas crecca
Family: Swans, geese, and ducks
A.K.A.: mud teal, greenwing, redheaded teal, common teal

Eye-catchers: Bobbing on the water like a spry little dinghy, the tiny green-winged teal seems dwarfed by most other ducks, particularly the mallard. The male's red head with bold emerald stripe identifies him in a crowd.

The male's gray sides show an almost pointillist pattern, and he has a yellow patch beneath his tail. His chestnut red head has an emerald stripe down the side. The female is a drab brown, and both sexes of this small duck have a characteristic green patch on the wing.

Natural History: In winter, a flock of greenwings gathered together on a pond makes for a noisy, busy congress. The males are all preening and fluttering, stretching their necks and fluffing their feathers. There is a low whistling din above the crowd as the ducks chatter. Then a pattern seems to emerge. This isn't just a flurry of preening, this is a show! All the males are performing the same set of actions, over and over. That preening and nervous fluttering is actually a greenwing courtship display. Ducks begin courtship early, sometimes in fall, though most often in late winter. Not ones to reinvent the wheel, ducks utilize a ritualized series of behaviors that all members of a species understand. Green-winged teals stretch their necks, rear up a bit, waggle their tails, fluff their wings, and give a repeated whistling call, *KRICK et!* This call is so distinctive it's represented in this duck's Latin name, *Anas crecca*.

Greenwings are among the smallest of ducks, but they use their small size to advantage. In flight, flocks of greenwings wheel and bank in tight formations like web-footed swallows, flashing suddenly right or left as they fly over a prospective pond, then settling suddenly on the water in a group. The female's contented voice sounds across the water, a series of four quacks descending in pitch—*QUACK, Quack, quack, quack*. Despite the tender, solicitous appearance presented by duck pairs as they court and swim side by side, after mating the male usually departs, leaving the female to build the nest, incubate the eggs, and brood the young. During incubation, when she must leave the nest to feed, the female carefully covers the eggs with down to protect them.

The **cinnamon teal** is another small, handsome duck, the male gleaming coppery bronze in the sun.

When and Where to See Them: Statewide September through April on freshwater ponds, lakes, and marshes and saltwater bays and estuaries.

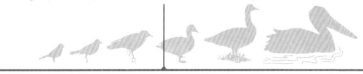

Green-winged Teal male

Cinnamon Teal male

Cinnamon and Green-winged Teals

MALLARD

Anas platyrhynchos
Family: Swans, geese, and ducks
A.K.A.: greenhead, curlytail

Eye-catchers: The familiar gleaming emerald head of the male mallard is its defining crown.

The male mallard is a large duck with an iridescent green head that appears dark blue or purple in some light. He has a yellow bill, white neck ring, chestnut breast, gray back, and curly tail. The female is a mottled brown.

Natural History: Have you ever passed by a pond and seen its surface covered with feathery duck rumps, all pointing toward the sky? Mallards are dabbling ducks, meaning they sit on the surface of shallow water and duck their heads under to reach aquatic plants, insects, and detritus in the mud, so it is a common sight to see them tipped "bottoms up."

If you can recognize no other duck in the wild, you ought to be able to recognize a mallard. This large duck with the hallmark green head is found throughout the Northern Hemisphere and is the ancestor of all breeds of domestic duck except the Muscovy. Indeed, mallards seem ready and willing to live closely with humans, taking up residence in parks, golf courses, even backyard ponds and swimming pools, and having no qualms about being hand-fed. The loud *QUACK, quack, quack* of the female mallard is the signature sound of ducks to most people.

To human eyes, the mallard pair makes a charming couple, swimming quietly side by side on the water, the male seeming attentive and solicitous of his mate. Then comes the actual mating act, which has startled many a naive viewer feeding ducks in the park. The male chases the female around, in and out of the water, finally climbing up on her back and pecking her head rather aggressively, pushing it underwater. Despite the surprise and shock of onlookers, the female is none the worse, shaking her head and paddling off once things are finished. Her mate departs once the eggs are laid. Soon after hatching the downy yellow-and-black ducklings follow their mother to water and swim dutifully behind her like a string of fluffy beads.

When and Where to See Them: Statewide year-round on freshwater lakes, ponds, rivers, and flooded fields, and in urban parks, ponds, and golf courses.

Mallard male

Flock of male and female Mallards

NORTHERN SHOVELER

Anas clypeata
Family: Swans, geese, and ducks
A.K.A.: spoonbill, broadbill

Eye-catchers: The shoveler's goofy spoon-shaped bill identifies it. Its bold blocks of color—green head, white and chestnut body—are easy to spot even at a distance.

The male shoveler has a green head, white breast, and chestnut sides with gray wings. The long bill is spatulate at the end. The female is a mottled brown.

Natural History: The shoveler looks like nothing so much as a cartoon character. The long bill, spreading into a comical spoon at the end, always seems about to catch in the water or trip its wearer. Despite its appearance, the shoveler's bill is a marvelous tool. As the shoveler feeds, it dabbles with its bill in the water or mud. Tiny "teeth" along the edge of the bill act like a micro-filter to strain out seeds, plants, and tiny aquatic animals. The bill is also equipped with a wealth of sensory nerve endings, which help the duck feel for edibles in the water and mud. With this sensitive filtration system, the shoveler can make a meal where ducks with cruder bills would go hungry. At times groups of shovelers feed cooperatively, swimming slowly one after another in a tight circle. The paddling of one duck stirs up mud from the bottom, which is strained for food by the next duck in line, who stirs up mud for the duck behind it, and so forth.

In fall and winter shovelers gather in huge flocks. Ponds and lakes of the Central Valley and around the Salton Sea may be covered with thousands or tens of thousands of shovelers.

When and Where to See Them: Statewide mid-August through April on freshwater ponds, lakes, and marshes and saltwater lagoons, marshes, and estuaries.

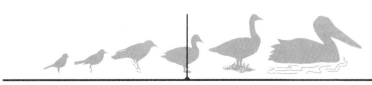

Northern Shoveler male

RUDDY DUCK

Oxyura jamaicensis
Family: Swans, geese, and ducks
A.K.A.: butterball, stiff-tail, bluebill

Eye-catchers: In summer the ruddy's bright blue bill and stiff tail identify him. At other times of year watch for the flash of those white cheek patches.

In summer plumage the male is cinnamon red with a dark cap, white cheeks, and bright blue bill. In winter he is gray but retains his white cheeks. The female resembles the winter male but with a dark bar through her white cheeks. The male's tail is often held up stiffly.

Natural History: Any time of year the pert little ruddy duck is a pleasure to watch puttering around on calm waters. Swimming with his stiff tail held up like a board, the ruddy looks like a deep-sided little boat. In spring and summer the male's bill is a bright sky blue and he busies himself with his courtship displays. Bobbing his head repeatedly he suddenly squirts a spurt of water at the object of his interest and gives a hoarse bleat. The ruddy is a diving duck, equipped with large feet set far back along its body to aid propulsion underwater. This leg placement means the ruddy cannot walk on land but must shuffle around clumsily. The ruddy's rounded wings are small for its weight, and to take off it must run pattering across the water's surface on its large feet. Thus the ruddy usually dives rather than take flight to avoid danger.

In winter the male ruddy duck loses his handsome cinnamon plumage and blue bill, adopting drab gray. But he is still easy to identify because of his white cheek patches and the dark cap that comes down to his eye line, giving the appearance of a hat pulled down low over the eyes. Ruddy ducks build floating nests of stems and leaves anchored to pond vegetation. Not only do ruddy ducks incubate and rear one or two clutches of eggs, they also lay their eggs in the nests of other ducks, leaving their young to be raised by others. Their eggs are very large, bigger even than the eggs of the mallard, a duck twice the ruddy's size. This great size probably helps the eggs to be accepted by the foster mother.

When and Where to See Them: Statewide year-round on freshwater ponds, lakes, and marshes. On saltwater bays and estuaries in winter.

Ruddy Duck family

Ruddy Duck male in winter plumage

BALD EAGLE

Haliaeetus leucocephalus
Family: Hawks and eagles
A.K.A.: Washington eagle, white-headed eagle

Eye-catchers: The bald eagle's white head is as distinctive as the white dome of the U.S. Capitol.

In its mature plumage, the bald eagle is a very large, dark brown raptor with snowy white head, white tail, hooked yellow bill, and unfeathered yellow legs and talons. Young bald eagles lack the white head and have mottled markings on the tail and underparts.

Natural History: Even the most jaded among us cannot help but be impressed at the sight of an eagle. These great birds of prey represent freedom and wildness to us as much as they did to the founding fathers, for an eagle cannot live hemmed in by cities. Their strength, size, and power make them a natural symbol for our country.

The bald eagle would not be America's symbol if Benjamin Franklin had prevailed. Calling the eagle a bird "of bad moral character and not fit to become America's national bird," he suggested instead the wild turkey for its intelligence and wiliness. In a way, Franklin wasn't far off the mark. Bald eagles often pirate prey from smaller raptors such as osprey, chasing the smaller birds until they drop their catch. The other bird does the work, and the eagle takes the spoils. Despite their larcenous habits, eagles are accomplished hunters and fishers. They will take small mammals but prefer fish, and their legs are unfeathered to reduce drag in the water, unlike the dryland-hunting golden eagle, whose legs are feathered to the toes. Eagles are primarily a winter bird in California, flying south from nesting grounds in Canada and Alaska to winter on northern California lakes and rivers.

Eagles are so large they aren't easily mistaken for hawks. Their perched posture is particularly upright. It is an odd sight at first to see a tree full of eagles, their large bodies and white heads dotting the trees like so many songbirds.

Though few bald eagles nest in California, you might witness their spectacular courtship flight before they depart for breeding grounds. The two

Bald Eagle

great birds soar and dive together on the wing, sometimes joining talons and tumbling hundreds of feet locked together. A mated pair stays together until one mate dies. Young bald eagles are often mistaken for golden eagles because they are all-brown. A bald eagle does not acquire its signature white head until it is four or five years old.

When and Where to See Them: Statewide from October to March on large lakes and rivers, especially in the Klamath Basin and northern half of the state. Occasionally in summer in mountainous northern habitats.

AMERICAN COOT

Fulica americana
Family: Rails and coots
A.K.A.: mudhen, white bill, pond crow, waterhen

Eye-catchers: A coot declares itself with loud squawking and gabbling and by the way its head pumps back and forth as it swims.

A black waterbird with a distinctive white, chickenlike bill.

Natural History: "Mudhen" is a good nickname for this waterbird, which seems to be more chicken than duck. Cackling and gabbling like farmyard hens, coots squabble noisily with each other, assaulting their neighbors with much splashing and fluttering of wings. Their bills, too, are more like a chicken's beak than a duck's bill, and their toes aren't webbed but have fleshy lobes. When the swimming coot kicks back, these toe lobes flare out to aid paddling, lying flat as the foot comes forward. Despite their resemblance to ground-dwelling chickens, coots live most of their lives on the water, swimming and diving as well as ducks.

Coots build floating nests of pond vegetation, firmly anchored among the reeds. Soon after hatching, the handsome babies—black with heads colored a rich red and red bills—swim after their parents, forming a bobbing fluffy flotilla. If threatened, the babies climb up on their parents' backs for a ride, the little heads of the young ones peeking out from under the adults' wings.

Coots are among the most widespread and abundant waterbirds in North America. They are most closely related to the rails, secretive birds that skulk along in the shallows, moving in and out of aquatic vegetation. The coots are the noisy, gregarious branch of the family. They are easy to see on the water, their heads pumping forward and back as they swim. They always seem to be squawking, and their takeoff from the water entails a splashy run across the water before final liftoff.

When and Where to See Them: Year-round statewide in freshwater marshes, lakes, ponds, and canals as well as urban parks and golf courses. In winter also in saltwater marshes and estuaries.

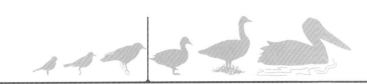

American Coot

SANDHILL CRANE
Grus canadensis
Family: Cranes
A.K.A.: blue crane, turkey crane

Eye-catchers: Its call, which sounds like a squeaky door and can be heard several miles away, and primordial profile identify this great gray crane.

A very large, blue gray bird with stilt legs, long neck, and a patch of red skin on the forehead.

Natural History: To see the milling flocks of sandhill cranes moving in the misty dawn light, or to watch as a trailing line of cranes flies overhead, great wings slowly beating the air, is to witness a piece of North America's past. These ancient birds—the crane family dates back in the fossil record 40 to 60 million years—once inhabited much of the marshlands of North America, but their numbers have been reduced by hunting and draining of their habitat for agriculture and development. Even so, when cranes gather in large groups, it is a wondrous sight. Their crackling calls, which sometimes sound like a loud trilling, can fill the air—*karroo, karroo, karroo.*

Cranes typically feed in grainfields and wet meadows by day, returning at dusk to the shelter of the open shallow water of wide riverbeds and marshes. Here they are better protected against the stealthy approach of predators. The evening fly-in and the dawn fly-out are quite dramatic, with the flapping and folding of large wings, the rustling of closely packed bodies, and the calling of hundreds or thousands of cranes. In late winter, as the time to depart for breeding grounds approaches, the cranes begin to dance. Here and there one bird, then another, bows and leaps or prances with wings outspread like a fan dancer. Two birds may leap from the ground together, touching breast to breast. Or a crane may pluck a bit of grass and toss it for its mate, a symbol of caregiving. This dancing seems to begin mate selection for young birds and reinforce the pair-bond of existing mates. Once on the breeding grounds, the courtship begins in earnest.

In flight, cranes can be distinguished from herons and egrets by profile. Cranes fly with their necks extended while herons and egrets carry their necks curved back in an S shape.

When and Where to See Them: From October to March in lowland grainfields, grasslands, and wet meadows of the Central Valley and southern and southeastern agricultural areas. They may be seen in flight almost anywhere during migration.

Sandhill Crane male (left), female (center), and immature (right)

KILLDEER

Charadrius vociferus
Family: Plovers
A.K.A.: chattering plover, killdee, pasture bird

Eye-catchers: The piercing scream of the killdeer—*kill dee dee dee!*—is unmistakable. You will also recognize its scurry-and-stop travel along the ground or beach.

Killdeer have a brown back with snowy undersides and two distinctive black rings on the throat and upper breast. In flight, the killdeer's white and dark brown wings flash boldly.

Natural History: A killdeer startled into flight is a bird not to be ignored. Wheeling and diving, flashing dark-light wings, the killdeer shrieks its name for all to hear. Unlike other shorebirds, the killdeer prefers upland habitat, nesting in meadows and grasslands often far from water. The "shores" this shorebird usually inhabits are the edges of freshwater lakes, ponds, rivers, and ditches.

If you've ever walked near a killdeer's nest, which is little more than a few pebbles scraped together on the ground, you may have become audience to this master actor. To draw predators away from its nest, the adult killdeer hobbles along the ground, dragging one wing as if broken and shrieking loudly. Once the potential threat is drawn far enough from the vulnerable nest, the wounded killdeer miraculously recovers, flying off with more shrieks of its piercing voice.

Killdeer adapt well to life around humans and often take up residence in urban parks and greenways, golf courses, athletic fields, and lawns. They will even nest on the gravel-topped flat roofs of buildings. Killdeer young are precocial, meaning they are "good to go" soon after hatching. Like puffballs on toothpicks, the downy young are soon out of the nest and following their parents.

When and Where to See Them: Year-round statewide at lowland freshwater lakes, ponds, and rivers, and in meadows, farm fields, parks, and suburban green spaces as well as estuaries.

Killdeer at nest

SPOTTED SANDPIPER

Actitis macularia
Family: Sandpipers
A.K.A.: teeter-bob, tip-up, teeter-tail, seesaw

Eye-catchers: Tipping forward and back, bobbing up and down, the spotted sandpiper scurries busily along freshwater beaches and shores.

In summer, the spotted sandpiper's brown back is barred with black and its snowy underside is dotted with telltale black spots. In winter the bird loses its spots and becomes quite similar to other sandpipers in winter plumage.

Natural History: Watch as the spotted sandpiper tips forward and back, bobs up and down, then scurries along a pond edge. No wonder country folk nicknamed this comical fellow "teeter-bob," "tip-up," and "seesaw." So widespread, familiar, and entertaining is this freshwater sandpiper (its summer range spreads from coast to coast and from Alaska almost to the Gulf of Mexico) that its list of colloquial nicknames goes on and on—"sand lark," "teeter peep," "river snipe," "peet-weet."

The spotted sandpiper is a maverick among its sandpiper cousins. Not only does it prefer freshwater habitats, it swims and dives, sometimes perches on wires, and may nest high in the mountains along lakes and streams. Unusual, too, is its love life. The females arrive first on breeding grounds, setting up territories and competing for mates as the males breeze in later. Females mate with more than one male and lay several nests full of eggs, which are incubated mainly by the males. The female also leaves hatchling care to her many mates, freeing herself to breed again.

Because spotted sandpipers are primarily winter birds in California, they wear their drab winter plumage here, making them appear much like all the other wintering sandpipers and shorebirds. The winter uniform is a gray back with pale undersides and few distinguishing markings. Watch for their odd, stiff-winged flight.

When and Where to See Them: Statewide in winter on beaches and sandbars of lowland freshwater lakes, ponds, streams, and wet meadows, sometimes at estuaries and ocean beaches. Also along southern coastal areas in winter.

Spotted Sandpiper in winter plumage

COMMON SNIPE

Gallinago gallinago
Family: Sandpipers
A.K.A.: jack snipe

Eye-catchers: Once flushed from cover, the snipe's fluttering flight and plump-bodied, neckless, long-billed flight profile identify it.

The snipe's stocky, short-legged body is a mottled brown. The head is boldly striped from front to back. The tail is quite short and the bill very long, giving the snipe a distinctive flight profile.

Natural History: You may think the snipe is a mythical bird that gullible green-horns are sent to catch with a gunny sack—the proverbial snipe hunt. But the snipe is indeed a real creature and, because of its shy habits, a treat to see. If you do chance to watch this freshwater sandpiper, with its short legs and very long bill, you'll notice how it rapidly probes the mud, stabbing up and down like a sewing machine. The snipe's bill is pliable and peppered with tactile nerve endings, allowing it to feel around for prey in the mud. The bill tip can bend to seize prey, like the tip of an elephant's trunk plucking a peanut.

Snipes are close cousins to the eastern woodcock. Because they spend their time directing their bills downward into the mud, snipes don't have much chance to keep an eye out for predators. Thus, their eyes are placed far around their skulls, so as they work with bill pointed down they still have a good view to the sides, behind, and above.

Not much of a songster, the male snipe instead produces an eerie flight sound called winnowing. Using its spread tail feathers as the violin and the air as a bow, the snipe flies great loops and figures in the air, strumming out an airy whistling—*whoo, whoo, whoo*—that rises and falls in pitch as the bird carves the air. Winnowing is most often heard over marshlands in morning and evening. This territorial display is performed mainly by males to put other male snipes on notice and to impress females. Sometimes female snipes may also winnow.

When and Where to See Them: In wet meadows and freshwater marshes and the grassy edges of ponds and streams. In summer in northern and northeastern California; in winter along much of the coast, in the Central Valley, and in southeastern valleys.

Common Snipe

RING-BILLED GULL

Larus delawarensis
Family: Gulls and terns
A.K.A.: common gull, lake gull

Eye-catchers: The black ring around the adult ring-bill's bill is a giveaway.

This sleek white gull has black-tipped gray wings, yellowish legs, and a yellow bill with a black ring near the tip. Young birds are a mottled brown.

Natural History: "Sea gull" is an inaccurate term for this most inland-dwelling of gulls. While it seems a gull's natural home should be a teeming harbor or rocky seacoast, the ring-billed gull is just as likely to turn up far inland on farm fields, lakes, and town dumps. Voracious eaters with indiscriminate appetites, they feed on small rodents, insects, birds' eggs and hatchlings, fish, garbage, and just about anything edible.

Gulls can be quite a challenge to identify because they take several years to attain their mature plumage. Ring-bills are a "three-year gull," meaning the mottled-brown young gull will not become a sleek white-and-gray adult-plumaged bird until three years old. Also, gulls change their appearance with the season, moulting from bright summer plumage to winter dress that is usually speckled or mottled. In winter the ring-bill's snowy head acquires brown freckles. Ring-billed gulls are most commonly seen in California in winter.

Another winter gull, the **California gull,** looks much like the ring-bill but the adult has both a black and a red spot on the lower bill instead of a black ring. Sometimes called a Mormon gull, the California gull is renowned in Utah for saving the Mormon settlers' first crop by arriving fortuitously to devour a plague of locusts.

When and Where to See Them: Statewide fall through spring, though mainly on lakes, rivers, farm fields, dumps, and urban areas as well as coasts, estuaries, lagoons, and harbors.

*Ring-billed
Gull*

*Ring-billed
Gull in
first-winter
plumage
(immature)*

California Gull

GREAT HORNED OWL

Bubo virginianus
Family: Typical owls
A.K.A.: hoot owl, cat owl

Eye-catchers: The hollow hooting of the great horned owl sounding in a woodland is a familiar night sound.

A big owl with large round head, large forward-facing yellow eyes, and two feathery tufts resembling horns on its head. The plumage is brown with black barring.

Natural History: Said to be supernaturally wise, to commune with evil spirits, or to portend death, owls have fascinated human cultures throughout the world since ancient times. Perhaps it is because of the owl's familiarity with the night, a world in which we daytime creatures lose our vision and our sense of security.

Great horned owls are perhaps the most familiar of owls, and the most easily seen. Their large, cylindrical bodies sit perched quietly in trees during the day, usually close to the trunk. At night their large shapes are often seen perched on poles, tree limbs, even buildings as they wait silently for prey. An owl's wings—large, wide, and very rounded at the tips—are well-adapted for night hunting. The primary feathers, those that are like "fingers," have serrated edges, allowing air to slip past the feathers without creating sound.

Of course the owl's large, human-size eyes are also important tools for hunting in the dark. Feathery disks around the face help reflect light into the eyes and also funnel sound to the owl's ears, like cupping your hand to your ear. Owls have no external ears, only openings on either side of the head. To help the owl hunt by using sound, the ears are asymmetrical, one higher than the other, so the bird can pinpoint sounds in both a horizontal and vertical plane. When an owl swivels and cranes its head, it is doing two things—adjusting the head to equalize sound to the ears, and trying to get a better look. Since its eyes are fixed in the sockets, the owl must move its head to adjust eye position.

Great horned owls hunt a variety of prey—mice, rabbits, even skunks, whose perfume they apparently cannot smell. These fierce, prolific hunters are sometimes dubbed "winged tigers."

When and Where to See Them: Statewide year-round in mixed and open woodlands, riparian areas, wooded canyons, desert oases, farms, and urban and suburban parks and yards.

Great Horned Owl

Young Great Horned Owls

BELTED KINGFISHER

Ceryle alcyon
Family: Kingfishers
A.K.A.: lazybird

Eye-catchers: With its punkish crest, oversized head, and heavy body, a kingfisher perched on a twig over water is hard to miss.

This handsome blue gray bird has a large head, wide white neck ring, long heavy bill, and a rough-cut crest. The white breast has a band of gray blue across the chest. The female has a second chestnut band across the belly.

Natural History: The kingfisher is not a hard bird to notice, announcing itself with a harsh, ratcheting cry as it flies up a stream course. Its flight profile is arrowlike, the head flattened, the long bill prominent, and the wings large for its body. Perched on a branch near the water, the kingfisher's profile is also unique. In fact, the kingfisher looks as if it were put together by committee—a head that looks too large for its body, a slanting flattop crest with the look of a bad haircut, a short neck, heavy bill, and tiny feet. Yet the kingfisher, true to its name, is good at its task, dropping down from a perch over water to grab small fish from pond or stream. To teach its young proper fishing technique, the adult kingfisher drops bits of fish into the water for the youngster to retrieve.

Kingfishers nest in long tunnels dug in a stream bank. The adults excavate the tunnel using their bills, kicking the loose mud out of the entrance in a spray of dirt. The tunnel slopes up as much as 20 feet to a nest chamber, the angle ensuring that water will not drain down into the nest. As the adults come and go at the entrance, their feet wear two grooves in the floor of the entry, a sure sign that a bank tunnel is the home of kingfishers.

When and Where to See Them: Statewide from late August through April along lowland streams, rivers, ponds, lakes, and freshwater marshes, sometimes along coasts. In summer in northern California near freshwater streams and lakes.

Belted Kingfisher male

BLACK PHOEBE
Sayornis nigricans
Family: Tyrant flycatchers
A.K.A.: black-headed flycatcher, western black pewee

Eye-catchers: Black-and-white formal attire distinguishes this flycatcher, as does its habit of pumping and spreading its tail.

The phoebe looks as if it has been dipped in black, all but the bright white belly and under-tail area.

Natural History: *Fee-bee, fee-bee, fee-bee* sounds from a tree along a stream, the calls sometimes stepping up in pitch on the second note, and sometimes stepping down. Perched on a lower branch, the songster is a handsome black phoebe, its plumage a study in crisp black-and-white. Peering about, the phoebe slowly pumps its tail up and down, indicative of its calm, tolerant temper. In classic flycatcher style, the phoebe sails out from its perch to grab a flying insect, looping back to the same spot to await the next tidbit.

Once they have defined a nesting territory, black phoebes may remain on it year-round. Quite tolerant of humans, they often inhabit farms and suburban parks, hunting insects over landscaping pools in backyards, livestock troughs, and irrigation ditches. Phoebes are never far from water, and their nests have even been found built several feet down inside wells. Their nests are sturdy cups of mud and plant fibers, securely glued on cliffs, buildings, and walls. Phoebes reuse the same nests in successive years, raising their young amid human activity with little concern.

When and Where to See Them: Year-round throughout the state in riparian areas, including ponds, streams, irrigation ditches, and watered canyons, with some southward movement in winter.

Black Phoebe

BARN SWALLOW

Hirundo rustica
Family: Swallows
A.K.A.: fork-tailed swallow, barn-loft swallow

Eye-catchers: Its classic swallowtail, forked into a deep V, identifies the barn swallow among others of its kind.

The back and wings of this handsome swallow are a gleaming blue black, the breast a rich brick red, becoming paler below. The long tail is deeply forked, with white spots sometimes visible.

Natural History: Like a stunt pilot, the barn swallow swoops and dives, wheels and banks, carving impossible arcs in the air, all at high speed. But these aerobatics aren't for show. Swallows feed on flying insects; as they swoop and wheel they are following their maneuverable prey and eating on the wing. To catch these insects, swallows must be better fliers than their prey, able to follow a moth or mosquito's evasive maneuvers. Swallows have mouths that open wide, creating a gaping maw with which they engulf prey. Bristles around the mouth also help, acting like a catcher's mitt to scoop food into the mouth.

So adapted are swallows to life on the wing that they even drink in flight, swooping down to scoop a sip from a pond's surface. Their bodies are slim, sleek, and aerodynamic, their wings long and pointed to help them cut the air and make sharp maneuvers. In addition to its handsome plumage, the barn swallow trails behind it a long, forked tail, the namesake for the gentlemen's jackets known as swallowtail coats.

The barn swallow has endeared itself to people, not only because it eats annoying insects, but for its sociability. Barn swallows readily build their nests under the eaves of barns and houses, raising their young as their human neighbors come and go below. The nest is a cup formed of mud pellets mixed with grass and plastered against a vertical surface.

When and Where to See Them: Spring through fall statewide in meadows, farmland, suburban parks and golf courses, city intersections (where they hunt insects), and freshwater marshes, lakes, and ponds.

Barn Swallow female (left) and male (right)

YELLOW-BILLED MAGPIE

Pica nuttalli
Family: Crows
A.K.A.: California magpie

Eye-catchers: The bold formal plumage of the magpie—black on white—is set off by this bird's distinctive yellow bill.

A large, long-tailed bird with a yellow crowlike bill, yellow skin around the eye, and dramatic black-and-white plumage that shines green and purple in the light. White wing patches flash in flight.

Natural History: The yellow-billed magpie is a true native of California, for this bird is found nowhere else in the world. Smaller than its more widespread cousin, the black-billed magpie, the yellow-bill has the same assertive style and loud raucous voice as the rest of the crow family. It is less timid of humans than the black-billed magpie, and more social with others of its kind, nesting in loose colonies, one nest per tree. A magpie nest is hard to miss, a large mass of sticks topped with a roof. From the correct angle you can see right through the nest, in one door and out the other.

Magpies travel the open country of the Central Valley searching for food. They are eclectic in their food choice, eating insects, carrion, fruit, grain, berries, or whatever they may find. Two birds contending over one bit of food may spar, pointing their bills up and butting chests until one yields. Once considered agricultural pests, magpies were subjected to intense efforts to eradicate them. Luckily these unique black, white, and yellow birds, such special Californians, survived and are now no longer persecuted.

When and Where to See Them: Year-round in farm fields, grasslands, and riparian woodlands of the Central Valley and interior valleys of the southern Coast Range, usually near water.

Yellow-billed Magpie

MARSH WREN

Cistothorus palustris
Family: Wrens
A.K.A.: cattail wren, reed wren, saltwater marsh wren

Eye-catchers: The up-cocked tail and long, curving bill identify a wren. A white eyebrow and black-and-white streaking on its back denote a marsh wren.

The marsh wren is warm brown above with black-and-white streaking, paler undersides, a white throat and breast, dark brown cap, white eyebrow, down-curved bill that is shorter than the head, and tail often held cocked up.

Natural History: What bird has a body profile like a teapot? A wren, with its up-cocked tail for the handle, plump body for the pot, and sloping head and down-curved bill forming the spout.

You will certainly hear the bright song of the marsh wren bubbling up from among the reeds and cattails, though the shy bird plays a game of hide-and-seek—he hides, you seek. You can't help but be charmed by his song, a succession of trills, rattles, gurgles, and rasps. Then the wren may suddenly fly straight up out of the marsh, fluttering and singing, before settling again in a new hiding place among the reeds.

Male wrens often build several dummy nests, perhaps to impress females with their abilities as home providers, but it is the female who actually weaves the nest that will hold her eggs. Lashing together the stems of reeds and cattails as supports, she fashions a round, coconut-shaped nest woven of sedges and cattail fronds, leaving a hole in the side as an entrance. Males frequently raid the nests of neighboring wrens, destroying the eggs, perhaps to eliminate nonrelated young that would compete with their own.

The **house wren** prefers drier habitats, often near human habitation. It comes readily to a well-placed birdhouse with an opening of one and one-eighth inches.

When and Where to See Them: In summer through much of the state in freshwater and brackish marshes, dispersing south in winter also into salt marshes and brushy thickets.

Marsh Wren

House Wren

RUBY-CROWNED KINGLET

Regulus calendula
Family: Kinglets
A.K.A.: ruby-crown, ruby-crowned wren

Eye-catchers: A gray green dough ball warbling a mighty song is the kinglet.

A tiny, plump bird, gray olive on its back and wings, paler and yellow below, with two white wing bars and a white eye ring. The male's red crown patch is seldom visible.

Natural History: The kinglet is a plump, round dab of a bird. Each large eye is surrounded by a white ring that makes the bird seem to be always staring. You will certainly hear the kinglet's full-throated warble enlivening a pine tree or thicket before you see the bird, which may take some searching. Once you find him, you may wonder how this tiny sprite can belt out such a fine, loud song.

Kinglets are busy bug eaters, fluttering among the foliage to pluck insects from branch tips, hovering like hummingbirds, or searching among leaf litter for ants, beetles, spiders, caterpillars, flies, and other invertebrates. They will drink tree sap and sometimes eat fruit and seeds.

Despite its name, don't expect to see the kinglet's ruby crown. The male saves his flashy top for special occasions. Like the wing patches of a red-winged blackbird, the kinglet's red crown can be covered or revealed by the bird. He flashes it when excited or to do visual battle with another male. Like tiny avian matadors, the kinglets bend their heads forward, erect their crown feathers, and flash red at their opponent.

When and Where to See Them: In summer in coniferous forests between about 6,000 and 8,000 feet in northern mountains and higher southern ranges. Statewide in winter and during migration in woodlands, suburban parks and gardens, farms, and desert oases.

Ruby-crowned Kinglet male

CEDAR WAXWING

Bombycilla cedrorum
Family: Waxwings
A.K.A.: cedar bird, cherry bird, Canada robin

Eye-catchers: The waxwing conveys elegance with its handsome crest, sleek gray green plumage, and proud bearing.

The waxwing is a sleek, greenish gray brown with a yellow belly, white under the tail, and a yellow band across the tail tip. The head has a crest and a black mask slanting upward across the eyes. The waxy red wing tips are often hard to see.

Natural History: Like classic wanderers, cedar waxwings roam the state, primarily in winter, showing up suddenly in a garden or woodland where fruits and berries are ripe, only to depart just as suddenly for somewhere new. Their travels are irregular; a site that brimmed with waxwings one year may not see a single one the next. Waxwings generally travel in flocks, so when one arrives it is soon joined by many. So great is the urge to be among others of its kind that even a nesting bird will leave its territory to feed with a flock of its fellows.

Waxwings travel where the winds of fate take them, with no set plan, always bringing much activity, noise, and excitement wherever they go. If waxwings should alight in your yard, it's quite an event. Suddenly the trees are filled with handsome, crested birds dressed in understated yet well-cut suits of sleek gray green, their eyes striped with an upturned line of black. Flying from tree to tree, the busy nomads call to each other incessantly. The cedar waxwing's fondness for juniper or cedar berries, an important winter food, along with the red tips of its wings, which look somewhat waxy, give the bird its name.

True to their nature, just when you have been totally charmed by these elegant birds, they move on without so much as a good-bye.

When and Where to See Them: Throughout the state in winter in a variety of habitats—dense forest, mixed woodlands, desert oases, suburban parks, gardens, yards, and orchards.

Cedar Waxwing

YELLOW WARBLER

Dendroica petechia
Family: Wood-warblers
A.K.A.: yellow bird, summer warbler, wild canary

Eye-catchers: A brilliant flash of yellow in the treetops announces the yellow warbler.

This bright yellow bird has an olive wash on its back, wings, and tail. The male has reddish streaks on his underside.

Natural History: A scrap of avian sunshine flits among the outer branches of a tree, working busily through the foliage picking insects from leaves and twigs. The yellow warbler is a delight both for its bright color and its energy. *Sweet-sweet-sweet, I'm so sweet* is the classic interpretation of the yellow warbler's cheery song. Another familiar warbler, the **common yellowthroat,** olive green with a bright yellow throat and black bandit's mask across its eyes, sings *wichity wichity wich.*

The yellow warbler is among the most widespread of American warblers. In summer it brings its yellow cheer to streamside thickets, woodlands, and gardens throughout most of the United States, Canada, and Alaska, to the edge of the Arctic Circle.

There is a dark side, though, to the yellow warbler's life. It is one of the most common birds to have its nest parasitized by the brown-headed cowbird. Cowbirds do not build their own nests but lay their eggs in a host nest. Cowbird babies usually hatch quicker and are larger than the host's young, thereby outcompeting them for food. Some yellow warbler populations are in real trouble because of loss of young to cowbird parasitism. So close is the relationship between yellow warblers and cowbirds that the warbler has evolved the ability to recognize the larger cowbird eggs as foreigners and defend against them. If the female warbler has laid no eggs, or only one, she builds a new floor in the nest, walling off the offending cowbird egg, then lays her eggs on the new floor. Yellow warbler nests have been found that contain as many as six floors. If, however, the warbler nest already contains eggs, the warbler accepts the strange egg, possibly because her own eggs are nearing hatching and have a better chance of surviving competition with the young cowbird.

When and Where to See Them: Largely statewide from April through August in open woodlands and thickets, particularly near water, from a few hundred feet in elevation up to about 9,000 feet. In migration they show up at desert oases, orchards, urban parks, gardens, and yards.

Yellow Warbler male

Common Yellowthroat female

Common Yellowthroat male

YELLOW-RUMPED WARBLER

Dendroica coronata
Family: Wood-warblers
A.K.A.: myrtle warbler, Audubon's warbler, butterbutt

Eye-catchers: This plump, gray warbler's yellow trim—on rump, crown, throat, and sides—identifies him.

In breeding plumage the male is charcoal with a bright yellow or white throat, yellow crown, yellow rump, and a yellow patch on each side. He is duller and browner in winter. The female is similar to the male but duller.

Natural History: Warblers are often challenging birds to see, but of all of them, the chances of seeing the handsome yellow-rumped are greatest. Dressed in charcoal gray with yellow points, the yellow-rumped warbler is the most abundant and widespread warbler in North America. It spends winter here instead of heading south like so many of its warbler kin.

Yellow-rumps are active birds, sitting in the tops of trees singing, flying out from a perch like a flycatcher after flying insects, foraging high and low in dense foliage, and even hopping on the ground like a sparrow. In winter they move to lower-elevation woodlands and open areas, forming loose, dispersed flocks. The individual birds keep in touch with each other with a constant chirp, as if to say, "I'm here. I'm here."

Two subspecies of yellow-rumped warbler are found in California, varying mainly by throat color. The more common Audubon's warbler, the western subspecies, has a yellow throat while the myrtle warbler, primarily a subspecies found in the eastern U.S., has a white throat. Ornithologists at one time classified these two as separate species, but they interbreed freely where their ranges meet.

Yellow-rumps are voracious bug eaters but particularly in winter will eat berries, come to feeder trays for raisins, and sometimes take suet from feeders.

When and Where to See Them: April through October in coniferous mountain forests all along the state, moving in winter to lower-elevation woodlands, residential landscaping, grasslands, and agricultural land.

Yellow-rumped Warbler male in breeding plumage

Yellow-rumped Warbler female in fall plumage

LAZULI BUNTING
Passerina amoena
Family: Finches
A.K.A.: lazuli painted finch

Eye-catchers: A flash of sky trimmed with white and cinnamon red is the male lazuli bunting.

The male lazuli bunting is a striking azure blue on his head, back, and throat, with a white belly, cinnamon red breast, and two white wing bars. The female is gray brown with a bluish wash to her wings, rump, and tail.

Natural History: You're hiking on a brushy hillside when a bit of bird flashes red, white, and blue as it wings past. Its colors aren't quite those of the flag, but are striking nonetheless. The lazuli bunting's color pattern is similar to a western bluebird's, but the hues differ. The bluebird is a deeper blue and its breast is more brick red.

The pronunciation of this bunting's common name has become almost a joke among birdwatchers—*la ZOOL lee, la zoo LEE, LA zhu LEE, LAZZ you lie*. Pronunciations vary by region and individual, and there is probably no one right choice. The word *lazuli* is Latin for "azure," an appropriate adjective for this remarkably azure blue bird.

A conscientious property owner, the male lazuli bunting diligently patrols his territory, proclaiming his rights in song from a series of song perches. He is an enthusiastic singer, offering a bright song that begins high and tumbles at the end, sometimes described as *sweet-sweet, chew-chew, seet-chew*.

When and Where to See Them: From April through August on brushy mountain slopes, in thickets, chaparral, and coastal scrub, often near water, west of the Sierra Nevada and in eastern deserts.

Lazuli Bunting male

SONG SPARROW
Melospiza melodia
Family: Sparrows
A.K.A.: silver tongue, bush sparrow, swamp finch

Eye-catchers: This sparrow's melodic song—a series of clear notes followed by a rich warble—announces its presence.

These brown sparrows have brown backs and wings, streaky breasts with a dark central spot, gray eyebrows, and dark stripes from the corner of the mouth down the neck.

Natural History: Though he may not be particularly handsome in appearance, the male song sparrow has a voice that turns heads. Hidden in a streamside thicket, his bright song bubbles out in a repeated series of single notes and warbles. So pleasing is the song sparrow's song that it has invited much comment. The first three notes are often compared to the opening notes of Beethoven's Fifth Symphony. According to Thoreau, country folk described the song as saying, *Maids! Maids! Maids! Hang up your tea kettle-ettle-ettle.* It is no surprise that the song sparrow's Latin name means "song finch with pleasant song."

The song sparrow is a highly variable species. At least 17 subspecies are identified in California. The song sparrow's streaked plumage varies from quite pale in the desert to very dark in more moist habitats. All song sparrows have a dark spot on the breast and a long tail that pumps up and down as they fly.

The female song sparrow hides her nest on the ground amid weeds and matted clumps of grass or a few feet up in a thicket or dense vegetation. Song sparrows are frequent victims of nest parasitism by brown-headed cowbirds, which leave their eggs in the sparrow's nest, usually resulting in the death of the song sparrow nestlings.

When and Where to See Them: Year-round in weedy thickets, chaparral, and dense brush, particularly near water, through much of the state.

Song Sparrow with young

RED-WINGED BLACKBIRD
Agelaius phoeniceus
Family: Blackbirds
A.K.A.: redwing, marsh blackbird

Eye-catchers: The scarlet wing patches of the male flash in dramatic counterpoint to its black plumage.

The male redwing is a handsome, jet-black bird with red wing patches edged in yellow. The female is a streaky brown.

Natural History: Walk near a cattail marsh or wetland and you'll likely be serenaded by the discordant symphony of red-winged blackbirds. The noisy music of male blackbirds sounds a bit like a family band made up of cymbals, washboard, and whistle.

The red patches on the male's wings are much more than decoration. He flashes his wings like proud battle colors to proclaim territorial ownership or to challenge an intruder. A low-status male, or one sneaking into another's turf, will hide his red patches so as not to create a stir. If his presence passes unchallenged he soon uncovers his red badges and begins to sing.

Redwings are very territorial and will challenge any intruder on their turf, be it bird, animal, or human. If a hawk or crow flies over redwing country it will likely be pursued and harassed by the smaller birds, which dive-bomb the hapless intruder, sometimes riding on its back and pecking at its head.

When spring arrives, males set up territories within a marsh. Even the tiniest moist spot or patch of cattails seems to attract a red-winged blackbird or two. Each male finds a prominent perch atop a cattail or other high spot and begins singing and flashing his scarlet wing patches. The females then set up their own territories within the males', select mates, and build nests woven among the stalks of aquatic plants, usually suspended over water.

The **yellow-headed blackbird** also nests in marshes, though it prefers to build its nest over deeper water.

When and Where to See Them: Statewide spring through fall in marshes, wet meadows, flooded fields, and the edges of lakes and ponds. Blackbirds withdraw from high mountains and northern areas in winter, gathering in flocks with other blackbirds in fields, pastures, urban parks, and yards.

Red-winged Blackbird male

Red-winged Blackbird female

Yellow-headed Blackbird male

Yellow-headed Blackbird female

BREWER'S BLACKBIRD
Euphagus cyanocephalus
Family: Blackbirds
A.K.A.: glossy blackbird

Eye-catchers: In the sun this blackbird acquires a glossy sheen of purple and green.

A blackbird with an iridescent purplish head, greenish black body, and yellow eyes. The female is a muted gray brown.

Natural History: While many bird species have suffered and fled in the face of human development, the Brewer's blackbird has benefited, feasting on insects, grain, and seeds in farm fields after plowing or harvest. They also follow cattle in pastures, picking up the insects kicked up by cloven hooves, sometimes standing atop the cattle's backs like a scene from the African veldt. Brewer's blackbirds are equally at home in suburban parks and yards and at feeders. Watch them as they scurry about busily, heads pumping back and forth. This versatility in seeking food explains their Latin name, which means "well-fed blue head."

Brewer's blackbirds are gregarious and nest in colonies of up to 20 pairs of birds. Their nests are cups built of grass, pine needles, and twigs, sometimes mixed with cow dung and lined with plant fibers and horsehair.

Continuing their sociable habits after the breeding season, Brewer's blackbirds flock together with red-winged blackbirds, cowbirds, and even starlings. These milling, noisy flocks may number tens of thousands of birds, descending on fields to feed in iridescent black clouds. At night the flock retires to communal roosts, some of which have been estimated to include millions of individuals.

Despite its name, the **brown-headed cowbird** is also a blackbird. Rather than build its own nest, the cowbird lays its eggs in the nests of smaller songbirds. Since this often results in death for the host bird's young, cowbirds have become a significant threat to the breeding success of some species.

When and Where to See Them: Statewide year-round in parks, golf courses, fields, pastures, yards, grasslands, and wet meadows.

Brewer's Blackbird male

Brewer's Blackbird female

Lesser Goldfinch nest
containing a large speckled egg
of a Brown-headed Cowbird

Brown-headed Cowbird male

BULLOCK'S ORIOLE

Icterus bullockii
Family: Orioles
A.K.A.: hammock bird, northern oriole

Eye-catchers: A flash of orange and black among riparian woodlands and a hanging pouch nest signal the presence of orioles.

This fiery orange bird has a black head and wings, black throat, and white wing patches. The female is olive yellow on her back, buffy below, and has white wing bars.

Natural History: You're walking along a stream when suddenly the trees come alive with noisy orange-and-black birds flying from tree to tree. You've entered the world of orioles, where life is like a carnival. Dressed in bright Halloween colors, the flashy males zip energetically among the branches, pausing in the treetops to break into a volley of whistles and chatters like carnival barkers. Among these striking birds there is a sense of energy, noise, and motion.

The oriole's nest is an amazing piece of avian engineering, a pendulous pouch 6 to 10 inches long hanging suspended from outer twigs that look surprisingly small for the job. The female weaves her nest of plant fibers and bark, ending with a product that looks rather like a long sock hanging from the tree.

The Bullock's oriole is the western counterpart of the Baltimore oriole. Ornithologists have had a hard time classifying these two birds, since they look fairly different yet sometimes interbreed. For a time both orioles were lumped together as two races of one species, the northern oriole, but they have now been split again into two distinct species.

Orioles are bug eaters, particularly enjoying caterpillars of various moths, beetles, and weevils, thus they are valuable pest controllers. They also enjoy fruit and will come to cut oranges set out for them. They sometimes sip nectar from hummingbird feeders. This fruit-loving sweet tooth means they also may raid orchards and gardens for fruits and berries.

When and Where to See Them: Statewide in deciduous riparian woodlands along streams, rivers, and canals and in watered canyons, arriving in late March in southern California and mid-April in the north, remaining through August and early September. Some remain year-round in southern California in suburban and residential landscaping.

Bullock's Oriole male

Bullock's Oriole female

AMERICAN GOLDFINCH

Carduelis tristis
Family: Finches
A.K.A.: wild canary, thistle bird, yellow bird

Eye-catchers: This butter-yellow bird with a black cap looks like a scrap of sunshine snagged on a twig.

A small songbird, in breeding plumage the male is bright yellow with a black forehead, wings, and tail. The female is olive with darker wings and some yellow.

Natural History: Bright describes not only the goldfinch's stunning yellow color but its cheery, twittering song and its behavior as it busily gathers seeds from roadside thistles. The goldfinch is often dubbed the "wild canary" for its color and the male's musical singing.

While we bemoan the spread of thistles and other roadside weeds, there is a bright side—they are the food of choice for goldfinches. In fact the goldfinch's genus name, *Carduelis,* means "thistle eater," so it's no surprise they come readily to thistle feeders. Some goldfinch populations nest later in summer than other songbirds to synchronize with the thistle seed crop. And while most seed- and plant-eating birds feed their youngsters insects for needed protein, goldfinches offer seed, predigested and carried to the nest in the parents' stomachs.

In mid- to late summer, goldfinches bob like little yellow ornaments on roadside weeds. Garden flowers such as cosmos, zinnias, sunflowers, coreopsis, asters, and others, if let go to seed, will attract their interest as well.

The female weaves a fine cup nest of plant fibers and thistledown, so tight it will catch and hold rainwater. If the nest fills, nestlings may drown, so the adult shields the nest with her outspread wings during a rain. The **lesser goldfinch,** with olive back, black crown, yellow breast, and white-streaked black wings, is just as fond of thistle as its American cousin but is less restricted to riparian habitats for nesting.

When and Where to See Them: Late March to October in northern California and year-round from Marin County south. Spring through fall in riparian areas and open woodlands, dispersing into shrublands, deserts, fields, and urban areas in winter.

American Goldfinch male
feeding on thistle seeds

American Goldfinch female

Lesser Goldfinch male

Lesser Goldfinch female

Anza-Borrego Desert State Park

Sage Grouse in Mono County with Sierra Nevada in background

Antelope Valley

BIRDS OF OPEN COUNTRY
Deserts, Grasslands, Chaparral, and Farmland

Turkey Vulture/
   California Condor
White-tailed Kite
Red-tailed Hawk/
   Red-shouldered Hawk
American Kestrel
Sage Grouse
California Quail/Gambel's Quail
Mourning Dove
Greater Roadrunner
Barn Owl
Burrowing Owl
Common Nighthawk/
   Lesser Nighthawk
Anna's Hummingbird/
   Costa's Hummingbird
Western Kingbird

Horned Lark
American Crow
Verdin
Bushtit
Cactus Wren
Wrentit
Northern Mockingbird
California Thrasher
Phainopepla
Loggerhead Shrike
Spotted Towhee/
   California Towhee
White-crowned Sparrow
Western Meadowlark
Great-tailed Grackle
Scott's Oriole/Hooded Oriole
House Finch

TURKEY VULTURE
Cathartes aura
Family: American vultures
A.K.A.: turkey buzzard, carrion crow

Eye-catchers: In flight, watch for the vast wingspan with wings held up in a slight V. Compared to hawks, vultures have very small heads.

This large, black, hawklike bird has very large, broad wings and a small, unfeathered, red head.

Natural History: The turkey vulture may seem an unpleasant bird due to its choice of foods: Vultures are scavengers, feeding on carrion and roadkill. Yet the role of the scavenger is an essential one ecologically, aiding in the "recycling" of dead animal material. It's no accident the vulture's rather skeletal looking, red-skinned head lacks feathers; this is a sort of personal-hygiene adaptation for a bird that inserts its head into the decaying carcasses of dead animals.

Some Native American people have traditionally revered vultures as messengers to the gods. As the vulture spirals higher and higher in the sky, finally disappearing in the heavens, it seems to commune with the divine. Indeed, the vulture is a prince of the air. To take off, a vulture makes several ungainly bounds, flapping vigorously, but once it gains altitude, it stays aloft by gliding on rising columns of warm air. The vulture's broad wings, spanning 6 feet, provide a large gliding surface compared to its body size. In flight its body falls at a slower rate than the rising air, allowing vultures to stay aloft for hours without flapping their wings.

On the wing, vultures can be discerned from hawks and eagles by their small heads and the slight V profile of their wings—hawks and eagles hold their wings on more of a flat plane. The turkey vulture's wings appear two-toned—dark on the leading half, which is bone and muscle, and light on the trailing half, which is mostly feathers through which light shines. A close cousin of the vulture, the **California condor,** is extinct as a breeding bird in the wild. This highly endangered species is the largest land bird in North America, with a wingspan of more than 9 feet, and is the subject of intense recovery efforts. A small number of captive-reared birds have been released at the Sespe Condor Sanctuary in Ventura County and near the Grand Canyon in Arizona.

When and Where to See Them: Statewide in large groups during fall and spring migration, year-round in the southern half of the state and in summer in the north, in open country, grasslands, deserts, mountain valleys, and agricultural land.

Turkey Vulture

California Condor

WHITE-TAILED KITE

Elanus leucurus
Family: Hawks and eagles
A.K.A.: black-shouldered kite

Eye-catchers: Watch for kites hovering over open fields. At a distance this kite appears white.

This dove gray bird of prey has charcoal wings, a white head and tail, black shoulders, a black smudge around the red eye, and a sharply hooked bill. The kite is falcon-shaped in flight, with long pointed wings, long tail, and black patches visible at the bend of the wings.

Natural History: The name of this raptor—"kite"—might make you ponder a chicken-or-egg question of whether the bird or the toy came first. In fact, the soaring toy on a string was named for the way it twists, dives, and rises in the air mimicking the graceful, acrobatic flight of these small raptors.

Kites are handsome birds, their plumage soft gray and white. Their dish-shaped faces and strongly hooked bills give them a dramatic, hawkish appearance. Yet kites are less aggressive than many hawks and their feet and talons are weaker, though certainly adequate to handle their small prey, mainly mice, insects, snakes, and lizards. Kites hunt above open country, hovering on rapid wings like helicopters, their legs dangling, then dropping suddenly on prey in the grass below. At times entire fields may be alive with the hovering shapes of hunting kites, looking a bit like enormous, predatory hummingbirds.

During courtship, a pair of kites performs an aerial ballet, circling slowly together in air. Then one bird flies below its mate, turns on its back, and the two clasp talons. While the female is on the nest, her mate does all the hunting for the family, feeding her not only as she incubates the eggs but until the young leave the nest. As if they need to do everything with panache, the male transfers his catch to the female in flight, he winging slowly past with prey dangling in his extended talons as she flies out to meet him and accept the food with her talons. After the nesting season, kites may gather in large groups numbering up to 100, roosting together in marshy, wooded areas. Unlike most raptors, white-tailed kites have benefited from conversion of habitat to agriculture, probably because of the resulting increase in rodents. White-tailed kites are rare in the U.S. outside of California, though a few inhabit south Texas.

When and Where to See Them: Year-round the length of the state, mainly in southeastern deserts and lowlands and hills west of the Sierra Nevada, in marshy, wooded bottomlands and adjacent meadows, orchards, and agricultural areas with windbreaks.

White-tailed Kite

White-tailed Kite kiting

RED-TAILED HAWK

Buteo jamaicensis
Family: Hawks and eagles
A.K.A.: redtail, hen hawk, mouse hawk, buzzard hawk

Eye-catchers: The red-tailed hawk's rusty red tail is its distinctive cachet.

This large hawk is generally reddish brown with a streaked, creamy breast and a speckled, reddish band across the belly. However, the plumage of redtails can vary greatly; some are mottled, pale, or very dark. The tail of the mature adult is chestnut red.

Natural History: No sound quite defines the wild spirit of the West like the scream of the red-tailed hawk. Starting high and shrill it slurs downward as if tumbling down a sheer rugged cliff—*Keeeeer!* This savage call is used as background in countless movies and television shows to suggest the call of the wild.

The red-tailed hawk is the most widespread and likely the most recognized hawk in North America, a familiar sight perched upon poles along country roads. The redtail lives in various habitats throughout the continent with the exception of dense, unbroken forest and tundra. Its preferred habitat is open country with scattered trees, which provide nest sites, roosts, and vantage points. The redtail can make a living in these varied habitats because its diet is eclectic. While preferring mice, rabbits, and other small mammals, this hawk will take just about anything that it can handle—skunks, porcupines, domestic cats, birds, snakes, lizards, even insects.

The sight of one or more redtails circling slowly in a wide sky is a familiar one throughout California. As the air warms in the morning, the birds flap up into the sky, catching the rising thermals that allow them to stay aloft, gliding on wide wings with scarcely a flap. From this vantage point they search for prey on the ground below. The hawk's vision is incredibly acute; "hawkeyed" is no unfounded expression. While humans have one fovea, or focus point, in each eye, hawks have two, allowing them to resolve clear images at great distances, images that to human eyes would be blurry or not visible at all.

The **red-shouldered hawk** is a smaller, slimmer cousin of the redtail, the undersides of the adult bird a very rusty red. It prefers wet meadows, marshes, and woodlands near water.

When and Where to See Them: Year-round statewide in open country, grasslands, desert, broken woodlands, and agricultural land.

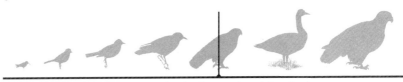

Red-tailed Hawk

Red-tailed Hawk in flight

Red-shouldered Hawk

AMERICAN KESTREL

Falco sparverius
Family: Falcons
A.K.A.: sparrow hawk, mouse hawk, grasshopper hawk

Eye-catchers: Watch for the kestrel's sideburns. You may see it hovering over open country, 10 or more feet above the ground.

This small, handsome falcon is striking in appearance. The male has blue gray wings, a rusty red back with black barring, peach breast with streaky spotting, and red tail. The female resembles the male, though her wings are rusty brown. Both sexes have two vertical stripes or "whiskers" down the cheeks, large eyes, and a short, hooked bill.

Natural History: The kestrel combines beauty and grace in both form and motion, all in a package not much larger than a robin. You may have passed by this small falcon many times as it sat above you on a power line or other perch, mistaking it for a songbird if you noticed it at all. But don't let the kestrel's small size deceive you. This hook-billed bird of prey is endowed with all the speed, power, and killing ability of its larger cousins. Its primary prey is grasshoppers and mice, found in the grasslands and open country that are its haunts. Kestrels often hover above the ground, working to pinpoint prey in the grass below before dropping for the kill.

Kestrels were used in the sport of falconry, gaining the nickname "sparrow hawk" because they were flown at small songbirds. While large hawks and peregrine falcons were the hunting birds of men, the trim and graceful kestrel was the bird of the aristocratic sporting lady. It must have made an elegant sight, the petite falcon perched with hauteur upon the gloved hand of a countess or queen, its demeanor every bit as aloof and haughty as that of its noble mistress.

Kestrels nest in tree cavities or other crevices and will use man-made nest boxes. The eggs are laid on the bare cavity floor without benefit of nesting material. The male kestrel often helps incubate the eggs, an unusual habit for birds of prey. Kestrels are also more vocal than many raptors. Listen for their excited *killy, killy, killy* calls.

When and Where to See Them: Year-round statewide in grasslands, agricultural land, desert oases, open woodlands, and sagebrush uplands.

American Kestrel male

American Kestrel female

SAGE GROUSE

Centrocercus urophasianus
Family: Grouse
A.K.A.: cock of the plains, sage cock, spiny-tailed pheasant

Eye-catchers: Most of the year grouse look like plump, combless wild chickens, but in spring the dancing males become the showmen of open country.

This large, plump grouse has streaky gray brown plumage and a black belly. The male has a long tail, white breast and collar, and black throat.

Natural History: The sage grouse is one of the most entertaining of birds, the male's courtship dance an absolutely fascinating display. Sage grouse gather on dancing grounds, called leks, where the males perform for the females, who choose a mate based upon this performance. Before dawn, the cocks fly or walk onto the lek, a large flat area where the vegetation is relatively short. The oldest birds take over the prime spots in the center of the lek, and they also do most of the breeding. The hens arrive and walk among the males, who begin their show. Each male fans his neck feathers, spreads his spiky tail like a bristling yucca, and lowers his wings, strutting back and forth impressively. Then comes the big bang of the show. Pausing, the male inflates enormous air sacs on his neck until they swell like an oversized white life preserver, engulfing his head and making him look a bit like a bloated, feathery beach ball. Then he expels the air with a popping gurgle. Over and over the cock repeats his display, his air sacs rippling rhythmically. A lek full of courting sage grouse sounds like the bubbling mud pots of Yellowstone National Park.

Sage grouse are aptly named. They feed on the aromatic leaves and buds of sagebrush, shelter beneath it, and also build their nests in its cover. In their travels across the West, Lewis and Clark shot a number of these grouse, calling them "the cock of the plains." But they found them to be unpalatable, the meat strongly flavored by sagebrush, the sage grouse's primary food. So important is the soft vegetation of the sagebrush to this grouse that it can't digest the hard weed seeds and grass grains that are important to many other ground-dwelling birds.

Both grazing and cultivation of the sage grouse's shrubland habitat have hurt this species, and its numbers have declined throughout its range.

When and Where to See Them: Year-round on sagebrush flats of the Great Basin and Modoc Plateau. Best opportunity for viewing the courtship display is a lek near Whitmore Hot Springs in Mono County, a California Department of Fish and Game wildlife viewing site.

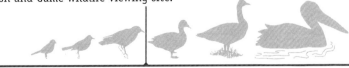

Male Sage Grouse displaying with ruff over head
and air sacs fully inflated, near Crowley Lake, California

Displaying male Sage Grouse

CALIFORNIA QUAIL
Callipepla californica
Family: New World quail
A.K.A.: California partridge, top-knot quail, helmet quail, valley quail

Eye-catchers: The California quail's plume curls forward from its head like a comma.

This gray, chickenlike bird is small and plump with a scalelike pattern on its sides and belly. A black-feathered plume protrudes from its head. The male has a black throat and white lines outlining its face.

Natural History: There is something wonderfully charming about these little quail, with their preposterous bobbing head plumes that look like the crowning glory of a sultan's turban. Familiar in chaparral, farmyards and fields, open woodlands, and suburban yards, where they will come readily to seed on the ground, these quail seem to percolate timidly from the vegetation, moving with their head-thrusting gait. Materializing in the open to search for food, they spirit away again into cover if alarmed. Their loud cooing calls, described as saying *chi-CA-go* or *who ARE you,* filter through the vegetation like music.

Quail are true ground-dwelling birds, running rapidly into cover when danger threatens, flying only as a last resort and then only for a short distance, the whirring of their wings a telltale sound of their departure. Young quail are ready to run on sturdy legs as soon as they have hatched and their down is dry.

This handsome, striking quail is the state bird of California. Despite its cautious nature, it is fairly easy to see because of its habit of coming into yards, gardens, and clearings seeking food. To see quail, sit quietly, patiently, and unobtrusively near a food source. The birds will emerge when the situation seems safe. Males may be seen perched on posts surveying their territory, posturing and calling. When the young have hatched, these gregarious birds form into coveys of several families. One of the males takes on sentinel duties, keeping watch from a stump or post while the rest of the group feeds. In winter coveys may number up to 200 birds.

A very similar bird, the **Gambel's quail,** inhabits the dry desert of southeastern California. It takes a close look, and a good field guide, to tell the Gambel's and California quail apart.

When and Where to See Them: Year-round through much of the state in chaparral, brushlands, open woodlands, suburban yards, parks and gardens, and edges of agricultural land.

*California
Quail male*

*Gambel's
Quail male*

*Gambel's
Quail female
with chicks*

MOURNING DOVE
Zenaida macroura
Family: Pigeons and doves
A.K.A.: turtle dove, wood dove

Eye-catchers: The dove's head-bobbing walk and mournful cooing call are unmistakable. You can't miss the whistling of its wings in flight and its white-edged, spade-shaped tail.

This grayish brown bird with a small head has a pinkish cast to its plumage, black spots on the wings, and an iridescent greenish purple sheen on the neck. In flight, the long tail is wedge-shaped with white edges.

Natural History: So sad and moving is the familiar cooing call of this dove that it reminds some listeners of the weeping of a loved one in mourning. Mourning doves mate for life, and the impression of them as devoted consorts is reinforced by their charming habit of sitting side by side, calling softly and rubbing their bills and necks together, the origin of the phrase "billing and cooing."

Mourning doves are highly adaptable, inhabiting grainfields, roadsides, weedy pastures, urban and suburban parks, gardens and backyards, open woodlands, hedgerows, even arid shrublands. Seeds comprise about 98 percent of their diet, thus the spread of agriculture, including conversion of forests and wetlands to fields and pastures, has benefited them. Mourning doves are found throughout the United States and are one of the most hunted game birds. They maintain their populations by their ability to live in proximity to humans and their fecundity—they may produce three or four clutches of eggs per season. Both adults incubate the eggs, the male generally taking the day shift while the female does her duty at night. Upon hatching, the young are fed a nutritious material called "pigeon milk"—regurgitated food from the crop of the adult, including material sloughed off from the stomach lining.

The mourning dove is distinctive in flight, from the whistling sound its feathers make to its striking cruciform profile of small head, stubby wings, and long, spade-shaped tail.

When and Where to See Them: Year-round statewide in open woodlands, desert oases, watered canyons, towns, suburbs, yards, parks, and gardens. In mountains and northern habitats in summer.

Mourning Dove

GREATER ROADRUNNER

Geococcyx californianus
Family: Cuckoos
A.K.A.: paisano, lizard bird, cock of the desert, snake killer

Eye-catchers: A large, long-tailed bird scuttling along the ground or across a road, its long tail pointing behind like an arrow, is a roadrunner.

This large, dark brown, ground-dwelling bird is flecked and streaked with white, with lighter underparts. The tail is long and pointed, the bill long, and the head topped with a shaggy crest. Patches of skin on the face are blue and orange, and the long legs are bluish gray.

Natural History: Forget *meep-meep* and the cartoon bird who survives the traps of Wile E. Coyote by virtue of luck and speed. The real roadrunner is a tough, savvy desert dweller adapted to survive in some of the most inhospitable terrain in the country. Truly a symbol of the Southwest, the roadrunner is always a delight to see. Hispanic settlers so admired this spunky hunter that shared their rugged world they nicknamed it *paisano,* or "country man." Its skills and courage, particularly its ability to kill rattlesnakes, were admired too by the native people of the Southwest. The roadrunner figures in stories and legends and is reputed to trap snakes within a corral of cactus spines.

Roadrunners are wonderfully adapted to the desert environment, feeding on snakes, lizards, scorpions, insects, and even the fruits of cactus. They will come to platform feeders, though perhaps seeking prey also attracted to the feeder rather than seed. The legs are long and well designed for running. Roadrunners have an unusual arrangement of toes—two face forward and two back, leaving a characteristic X-shaped track. In cold winter temperatures, roadrunners make use of solar heating by lifting their outer feathers to expose dark underplumage to the sun. In summer heat, they rest in cover during the hottest part of the day, compressing their feathers to reduce air pockets that might trap heat. By fluttering their throat skin to draw more air across their respiratory membranes, roadrunners cool themselves using evaporative cooling.

The courtship of roadrunners is quite a sight. The male lifts his head and parades for the female, wings and tail drooped and dragging, then bows with tail fanned and wings beating up and down. Once mated, the roadrunner pair defends its territory throughout the year.

When and Where to See Them: Year-round in chaparral, brushy areas of deserts, foothills, agricultural land, and dry woodlands, primarily in the central, southern, and southeastern parts of the state.

Greater Roadrunner

BARN OWL

Tyto alba
Family: Barn owls
A.K.A.: golden owl, monkey-faced owl, church owl

Eye-catchers: If you should encounter a barn owl, you will know it by its curious heart-shaped "monkey face."

The barn owl is slim, its plumage pearly white with some tan streaking. Its face is heart-shaped.

Natural History: It is an eerie and wonderful experience to enter an old barn or other structure and discover a cluster of heart-shaped barn owl faces peering down at you. These beautiful pale-golden birds adapt well to life around humans, taking up residence in barns, silos, church steeples, and other old buildings. Before the abundance of human structures, barn owls lived in caves, burrows, tree hollows, or within thick foliage. Barn owls are birds of open country. They are consummate nighttime hunters, flying softly and mothlike on wide, silent wings. Studies of the hunting abilities of barn owls revealed they can successfully hunt exclusively by sound. Researchers placed barn owls on perches in totally darkened rooms, then released mice on the floor. The owls pinpointed the mice by their scratchings and squeakings, then struck accurately to within a fraction of an inch (any slight variance from dead center is made up for by the owl's widespread talons).

Barn owls belong to a different group of owls (barn owls) than other North American owls (typical owls); in fact, they are the only species of the barn owl family found in North America. They live throughout the warmer reaches of the continent and are particularly abundant in southern California. Barn owls have a number of physical traits that vary from the other owls, but the most obvious is the heart-shaped ruff of feathers around the face. Great horned and other owls have round ruffs. A barn owl doesn't hoot but screams, hisses, chuckles, clicks, and when alarmed snaps its bill. Encountering an intruder, the barn owl sways its head from side to side. An entire barn owl family peering from a perch with necks extended and heads weaving is an arresting sight.

When and Where to See Them: Year-round statewide in lowlands and foothills near marshy meadows, grasslands, agricultural land, and town and suburban edges.

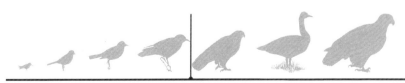

Barn Owl

BURROWING OWL

Athene cunicularia
Family: Typical owls
A.K.A.: ground owl, billy owl, howdy owl

Eye-catchers: If a small, brown owl flies up suddenly from a field or irrigation ditch, it is likely to be a burrowing owl.

This small, brown owl is flecked and streaked with white and has a dark collar and white eyebrows. It has a round head, long legs, and very yellow eyes.

Natural History: The burrowing owl is not most people's idea of an owl. It lives in burrows in the ground instead of in trees. It doesn't hoot. It is active during the day. This owl is one that has adapted to life in open country. With few trees in such terrain, it nests in the burrows of prairie dogs and ground squirrels, hunting grasshoppers and insects as well as occasional mice, prey that are abundant in fields and open grasslands.

Burrowing owls are a delight to watch, little round-headed birds standing on the ground on skinny stick legs. In spring, the courting pair of burrowing owls sits side by side at the entrance to the burrow they have chosen to nest in, rubbing their heads and bills together and calling softly. They stretch their wings and legs, comically standing on one foot with the other long, yellow leg stuck out sideways. After the young owls have emerged from the nest burrow, they cluster about the entrance, their large, round yellow eyes staring, heads bobbing and weaving as they try to focus on their surroundings. Burrowing owls don't hoot, though they coo softly. When disturbed in their burrow, they make a rattling sound that mimics the alarm rattle of a rattlesnake, certainly an effective deterrent to make a potential predator think twice about disturbing them.

The agricultural land of the Imperial Valley is a particularly good place to see burrowing owls, both in plowed fields and along the many irrigation ditches where they shelter in burrows in the banks. They are often visible day or night, perched in fields, on roadside banks, or flying along roadways. Burrowing owl numbers have declined throughout California, perhaps due to pesticides and disturbance of their habitat.

When and Where to See Them: Year-round primarily in central and southern California, along irrigation dikes and ditches, grasslands, deserts, and open, broken country. Especially common in Imperial Valley agricultural areas.

Burrowing Owl at burrow

COMMON NIGHTHAWK

Chordeiles minor
Family: Nightjars
A.K.A.: booming nighthawk, bullbat, moth hunter, will o' the wisp

Eye-catchers: In flight, the nighthawk's falconlike profile and bold white wing bars are very distinctive.

The nighthawk is a dark brownish black mottled with white. It has a blunt head, long notched tail, and long, pointed, tapering wings with broad white bars at the wrists.

Natural History: On summer evenings nighthawks put on a marvelous aerial song and dance act. Flying patterns in the air, winging high and low as they pursue insects, the birds repeatedly sound a distinctive, nasal *beent!* Then a high-flying nighthawk suddenly plummets to the ground, pulling up in a J-pattern and sounding a loud, airy *schoomp*. This dramatic sound display, sometimes called booming, results from wind rushing and vibrating through the primary ("fingertip") wing feathers and is linked to courtship, though nighthawks will boom throughout spring and summer. At times two nighthawks will fly close together, one shadowing the other as they flit this way and that like fast-flying moths.

Nighthawks aren't hawks at all, but members of a small family of evening- and night-hunting birds that pursue insects on the wing. The nightjar family, which includes the whip-poor-will and poorwill, gets its name from its members' jarring nighttime calls. The common nighthawk's Latin name translates roughly as "evening harp" or "stringed instrument."

Nighthawks share some physical characteristics with other eaters of flying insects such as swifts and swallows. They have small bills but wide, gaping mouths to make the job of engulfing flying insects a little easier. They often drink on the wing, swooping down to skim the water's surface. Like swifts they have small, weak feet, a characteristic of birds highly adapted to life in flight.

A smaller cousin, the **lesser nighthawk,** inhabits the Southwest, nesting from central California south. Only very close inspection will distinguish it from the common nighthawk—it is smaller and browner and the white wing bar is closer to the wing tip.

When and Where to See Them: Early June through mid-September mainly in central and northern California and west of the Sierra Nevada, in meadows, sagebrush flats near open coniferous woodlands, and near towns and suburbs.

Common Nighthawk male

Lesser Nighthawk

ANNA'S HUMMINGBIRD

Calypte anna
Family: Hummingbirds

Eye-catchers: Watch for the spectacular flash of rosy magenta when the male hummingbird turns his head into the light.

Both male and female are iridescent green. The male has an iridescent rosy red crown, face, and throat with red gorget projecting on either side of the head. The female is pale and lightly spotted on her underparts.

Natural History: Hummingbirds are primarily birds of the tropical forests of Central and South America, but the Anna's hummingbird is a true North American, and a Californian to boot. The Anna's lives year-round in the U.S. and nests almost exclusively in the Golden State.

A garden visit from an Anna's is a treat, the tiny shimmering bird flashing metallic green in the sun, with a jeweled rose red throat and crown. Truly seeming like a royal jewel, the Anna's hummingbird is aptly named in honor of Anna, the duchess of Rivoli and the wife of a prince. Hummingbirds are especially attracted to red tubular flowers, and a garden planted with "hummingbird plants" will attract these fascinating birds.

Hummingbirds are amazing aerialists, able to fly forward, backward, and upside down (in brief maneuvers), and stop abruptly and take off in an instant. Their ability to hover in place at a flower while feeding—by paddling their wings rapidly forward and back in a figure eight—is fascinating to watch. It surprises many people to learn that hummingbirds also eat insects, catching them on the wing or picking them from tree bark.

Imagine a tiny Japanese sake cup covered in spider silk and cattail down and you have an idea of a hummingbird's tiny nest. The female weaves the nest, hovering above and below as her long, narrow bill works busily like a sewing machine needle. The two tiny eggs she lays are the size of grapefruit seeds. With the long bills of the baby hummers poking skyward, the nest bristles like a pincushion.

The smaller **Costa's hummingbird** inhabits dry brushlands, deserts, and suburban yards and gardens in southern California. The male Costa's has a gleaming purple gorget that extends down either side of the neck like a drooping mustache.

When and Where to See Them: Year-round in central and southern California in chaparral, oak and riparian woodlands, agricultural areas, suburban parks, yards and gardens, mainly west of the Sierra Nevada.

Anna's Hummingbird male

Costa's Hummingbird male

Costa's Hummingbird female on nest, incubating eggs

WESTERN KINGBIRD

Tyrannus verticalis
Family: Tyrant flycatchers
A.K.A.: Arkansas kingbird

Eye-catchers: A gray, yellow-bellied robin-size bird that loops out and back from a perch is likely a western kingbird.

The kingbird's gray back, wings, and head contrast with its dark tail and sulphur yellow belly. The tail's outer edges are white.

Natural History: Kingbirds belong to a family of birds known as tyrant flycatchers. "Tyrant" may seem an odd term to use in reference to a group of songbirds, but the kingbird and its cousins are named for their aggressive hunting style. They take up a perch on a twig, post, or fence wire near open country, sallying out to snag flying insects, then looping back to the same perch. Sometimes they snap at their prey so fiercely you can hear the click of the bird's bill. Kingbirds are also aggressive toward other birds. Most dramatic is the kingbird's habit of attacking and driving away hawks, crows, and larger birds that venture into kingbird territory. Several kingbirds may gather together to mob and chase away the intruder, sometimes one of the kingbirds even riding on the hawk's neck, pecking at the raptor's head. The kingbird's voice is in keeping with its harridan behavior, a shrill, metallic twitter that sounds like a tape on fast-forward.

Kingbirds are fairly sociable with others of their kind, sometimes two or more pairs nesting together in the same tree. They are dutiful parents, teaching their young how to hunt and what prey to choose by catching insects and releasing them for the young to catch. A group of kingbirds gathered together after the nesting season is a noisy, active crew, chasing each other from tree to tree with much calling.

When and Where to See Them: Mid-March through mid-September over much of the state in grasslands, shrublands, and open country with scattered trees and woodlands. Their arrival from wintering areas in Central America is a harbinger of spring in California.

Western Kingbird

HORNED LARK

Eremophila alpestris
Family: Larks
A.K.A.: shore lark, prairie bird, road trotter

Eye-catchers: The male horned lark is rather nondescript, until he erects the little black "horns" on his head. Watch also for the pattern of black lines on the face and the tinkling call, often heard from overhead.

This grayish brown bird sports a pale yellow throat, black chest collar, black stripes on the head, and a black "mustache." Its small, black "horns" are actually tufts of feathers and aren't always visible.

Natural History: A drab, brown bird scurrying about dry, flat ground, the horned lark is not apt to attract a great deal of attention or admiration. But if you should witness the male's marvelous spring courtship flight, you'll have a new appreciation for these prairie larks. Typical of songbirds adapted to life in open country where there are few trees and thus few song perches, the horned lark has evolved a song display, called larking, that is performed on the wing. With bursts of wing beats, the courting male flies up in the sky to a great height. There he carves circles in the sky, his bright, twinkling song filling the air. At the end of his song, he folds his wings and plummets earthward, pulling up at the last moment.

Unlike sparrows, horned larks walk on the ground instead of hopping. They are able to make a living on bare, hard ground where few other birds venture. They forage for weed seeds, waste grain, and during summer, grasshoppers, grubs, and other invertebrates. Horned larks weave grassy nests on the ground, sometimes in the open or sheltered by a clod of dirt or clump of vegetation.

Horned larks are abundant in winter in California, gathering in very large flocks to feed on bare, gravely ground, sometimes in gravel parking lots if they are adjacent to weedy fields or roadsides. A feeding flock of horned larks is an interesting crew, all milling about, the males flicking up their feathery horns in a threat to bump their neighbor over, the neighbor flicking at the next, and so on.

When and Where to See Them: Widespread in the state in summer on sagebrush flats, grasslands, plowed fields, desert scrub, and other open terrain with short vegetation. Year-round on these habitats at lower elevations.

Horned Lark in winter

AMERICAN CROW
Corvus brachyrhynchos
Family: Crows
A.K.A.: common crow, corn thief

Eye-catchers: You can tell a crow from a raven by the crow's smaller size and squared-off tail, visible in flight.

Crows are large, jet-black birds with long, sturdy beaks. Their plumage is an iridescent purple in the sun.

Natural History: Crows are among the most familiar birds in North America. Outfitted in glossy black, they not only live in rural areas but have adapted well to urban and suburban life, roosting along power lines, on buildings, and in urban landscaping. Consummate opportunists, they have learned to find food in the city where they can—garbage, roadkill, pet food.

A crow's harsh voice may not be melodious like those of other songbirds, but crows are accomplished mimics. They can reproduce the calls of other birds and animals, mimicking the barking of dogs, crowing of roosters, even the crying of children and human laughter. Tales of the intelligence and abilities of crows are many—stealing shiny objects, flying off with chicken eggs, solving problems to get to food, even mocking scarecrows by roosting on them. A crow that frequented one family's yard would tease the family dog, dropping things on the dog's head, stealing its food, and confusing it by barking and meowing. The poor dog would go tearing around the yard barking at the unseen intruder as the crow perched overhead.

Crows can solve puzzles, quickly associate symbols and sounds with food, perform amazing tricks of memory, and even count to three or four. The crow family as a group is likely the most intelligent among birds.

Crows are often seen hanging out in groups, seemingly ripe for mischief. Just watch a bunch of them lined up on a phone wire, cawing, flaring their feathers, maybe performing feats of daring like hanging by one foot. American folklore and Native American legends are filled with crows as hucksters, ne'er-do-wells, and troublemakers, though they are also often depicted as prophets and wise creatures.

When and Where to See Them: Year-round over much of the state in open woodlands, agricultural areas with tree stands and windbreaks, orchards, and urban and suburban areas. In summer also in high, cold northern areas.

American Crow

VERDIN

Auriparus flaviceps
Family: Verdins
A.K.A.: goldtit

Eye-catchers: You will know this busy desert sprite by the way it flits among the desert scrub, clothed in yellow and gray.

This tiny bird is gray with a bright yellow head and throat. The female is paler than the male.

Natural History: Just when you think the heat of the desert must sap all energy from every living thing, you come upon a verdin, flitting busily about a mesquite tree or other desert shrub. The verdin may seem like the sort of bird only serious birdwatchers pay attention to, but once you recognize one, with its smart plumage of yellow and gray and its energetic demeanor, you will be charmed by its *joie de vivre*.

The verdin shares with its cousins the chickadees and titmice the type A personality of the truly driven, flitting about in constant search of food, at times clinging upside down to reach a tidbit. Verdins feed on insects, larvae, and occasionally berries and fruit. The verdin's call, too, is chickadee-like, a rapid *tsit, tsit* or *tsee-too-too*. The verdin's whistling song is surprisingly loud and carries quite far for such a bit of a bird.

Verdins are true desert dwellers, nesting among the mesquite and creosote. The male builds several nests, and the female chooses the one that pleases her. The nest is a large ball of thorny twigs, lined with spider's web and down. Verdins also build similar nests for secure winter roosting. Verdins can live in dry deserts, where there is little competition from other birds, because they do not need to drink water, obtaining their moisture from the food they eat. Like a wise desert rat, they are active in the coolest times of day, resting and seeking shelter during times of highest heat. Nests built early in the season, when temperatures are cool, are oriented with the entrance away from prevailing winds; nests built later face the wind to help cool the interior.

When and Where to See Them: Year-round in the desert regions of southeastern California, especially among desert scrub growing along dry washes.

Verdin

BUSHTIT

Psaltriparus minimus
Family: Bushtits
A.K.A.: coast bushtit, black-eared bushtit

Eye-catchers: The bushtit's tiny size, nondescript plumage, and energetic behavior define it.

This tiny, gray bird with paler undersides has a short bill and long tail. The male has dark eyes, the female cream-colored eyes. Males along the coast have a brownish cap, and some interior males have a black eye stripe.

Natural History: A bushtit is not a flashy bird. Dressed in dove gray plumage with no defining field marks or colors, it is still a charmer by virtue of its tiny size and industry. One of the smallest songbirds in North America, the bushtit is among the busiest and most energetic. Bushtits are sociable and friendly, flocking with other bushtits as well as chickadees, titmice, and wrens. After the nesting season, groups of as many as 50 birds may drift through an oak, piñon, or other woodland, twittering in high-pitched voices as they comb the foliage for insects, seeming like a chatty klatch of avian munchkins. The bushtit's Latin name means "tiniest lute player," a salute to its twittering voice. In cool weather a flock of bushtits huddles together for warmth in a mass of feathered bodies.

Bushtits are quite tolerant of the presence of humans, perhaps because we are too large to even be noticed by these tiny birds. Bushtits build hanging nests in the shape of gourds, woven of twigs, moss, and plant fibers. Once the eggs are laid, both adults will roost in the hanging pouch, taking turns incubating the eggs.

When and Where to See Them: Year-round through much of the state in a variety of brushlands and woodlands—oak thickets, piñon-juniper, and chaparral. They are rare in southeastern deserts.

Bushtit female (left) and male (right) building nest

Bushtit female

CACTUS WREN
Campylorhynchus brunneicapillus
Family: Wrens
A.K.A.: brown-headed cactus wren

Eye-catchers: The cactus wren's harsh voice—*cha! cha! cha!*—announces its presence in the desert landscape.

This large wren has a reddish brown back streaked with white, dark brown cap, bold white eyebrow, brown wings and tail barred with white, and speckled, pale undersides.

Natural History: Those familiar with wrens are often surprised at the unusual characteristics of the cactus wren, as if life in the hot, dry deserts of the Southwest have taken much of the wren-ness out of it. First, the cactus wren does not hold its tail cocked up as other wrens do. Next, unlike the bubbling trills of other wrens, or the melodious cascading voice of its southwestern cousin, the canyon wren, the voice of the cactus wren sounds as dry and thorny as the desert vegetation, rasping out a harsh, scolding *cha! cha! cha!* And while other wrens often adopt a stooped-over posture, tails in the air, the cactus wren is as likely to be seen perched fairly upright. Finally, the cactus wren is larger and fuller-bodied than its petite cousins.

Cactus wrens are well adapted for desert life. They build bulky, football-shaped nests woven of grass and twigs and set among the spines of cholla, catclaw, and other thorny desert plants. Sturdy and well built to withstand the surrounding thorns, the wren's nest may be as much as a foot wide, with a side entrance to allow safe passage through the spiny vegetation. Inside, the nest is lined with soft down and animal hair. The wren pair may raise as many as three broods a year; as the female incubates one clutch of eggs her mate may be working on construction of the next nest. Cactus wrens use these nests not just to raise their young but as shelter at other times of the year.

Cactus wrens often feed on the ground, turning over leaves and small stones with their bills as they search for insects and other prey.

When and Where to See Them: Year-round in deserts, valleys, and coastal sage scrub of southern and southeastern California.

Cactus Wren

WRENTIT

Chamaea fasciata
Family: Old World warblers
A.K.A.: Gambel's wrentit

Eye-catchers: The wrentit's whistly song, speeding up to a trill, sounds like an engine putt-putting slow then revving up to a purr.

This tiny, round bird is grayish brown above and cinnamon brown below, with prominent light eyes and a very long, rounded tail.

Natural History: The wrentit lives only along the Pacific Coast, in chaparral, coastal scrub, shrublands, and even suburban gardens, from Baja California to Oregon. While not an uncommon bird, the wrentit is so shy and elusive, its scrub habitat so dense, and the bird itself so drab and tiny that one might spend hours seeking it without a glimpse. On the other hand, the wrentit's loud song, a series of whistles accelerating into a trill—*peep, peep, peep, pee, pee, peepee-prrr*—is easily heard, teasing the birdwatcher who seeks the hidden singer. So loud and common is the wrentit's call that it frequently turns up in the background in soundtracks of movies shot on location in California.

At times the wrentit overcomes its shyness and emerges in the open. Once you do get a glimpse of a wrentit, you might think you're seeing a tiny ball of dough, stuck with long tail and pointed bill, and rolled in feathers. As it forages among the foliage for insects, grubs, and berries, it cocks its tail repeatedly like a wren. Though unrelated to either wrens or titmice, the wrentit bears its name because it shares those busy birds' nervous habits. The wrentit's Latin name translates to something like "ground dwarf."

Though seldom seen, the wrentit mated pair make a charming couple. They mate for life, taking up housekeeping within about a two-and-a-half-acre square bit of brushland that they seldom leave. They preen each other's feathers, forage together, and roost side by side, leaning so close together they look like a single ball of feathers.

When and Where to See Them: Year-round in hilly scrublands, brushlands, and chaparral the length of the state, mainly in the western half.

Wrentits

NORTHERN MOCKINGBIRD

Mimus polyglottos
Family: Mockingbirds
A.K.A.: mimic thrush, mocker

Eye-catchers: Watch for the flash of white wing patches and the white edges of the tail when the mockingbird flies.

About the size of a slim robin, the mockingbird is gray above and paler gray below, with a slender bill and long tail. Prominent white patches on the wings and white tail edges are visible in flight.

Natural History: The mockingbird is easily outclassed by other birds in the bright color and flashy plumage department, but when it comes to song, the mockingbird is in a class by itself. Other birds may have prettier songs, but the mockingbird wins out for versatility and vocal repertoire. Its Latin name means "many-tongued mimic," an apt description for a bird that has proven it can mimic the calls of 32 different birds in 10 minutes. It has also been known to re-create such diverse sounds as a chirping cricket, a croaking frog, the chords of a piano, a barking dog, and the squeaking of a wheelbarrow. So good are the mockingbird's versions of other birds' songs that electronic analysis can pinpoint no differences from the originals.

The mockingbird isn't just good at his job, he is also a willing singer. The male sings night and day, from a perch or even in flight. Close to the nest he sings a soft, whispering song.

In contrast to their image as amiable songsters, mockingbirds can be quite feisty in defending their territories. Neighboring males will meet up at the boundary between their turfs—obvious to them if not to us—and spar like tiny roosters, hopping sideways with head and tail held high, then darting at each other, forward and back.

Mockingbirds feed on grasshoppers, beetles, and other insects, as well as a good deal of berries and wild fruits. A hunting mockingbird moving about on the grass has the odd habit of suddenly extending its wings like an angel, probably a strategy to flush insects by flashing the white patches on its wings.

When and Where to See Them: Year-round in desert scrub, chaparral, brushy areas, agricultural lands, and parks, yards, and gardens in urban, suburban, and town settings.

Northern Mockingbird

CALIFORNIA THRASHER

Toxostoma redivivum
Family: Mockingbirds
A.K.A.: Sonoma thrasher

Eye-catchers: You'll know the thrasher from its scimitar bill and habit of scuffling about on the ground among the leaf litter.

The California thrasher is dark brown with a paler breast and cinnamon belly, pale eye stripe, long legs and tail, and a very long, down-curved bill.

Natural History: The California thrasher is well named, as it lives primarily in our state. It seems perfectly designed for the dry chaparral and shrub habitats where it lives. With long, strong legs, the thrasher spends much of its time on the ground, rustling in the leaf litter like a homeowner pawing through a cluttered closet. A rustling in the underbrush will often herald a brief opportunity to glimpse this long-billed, long-tailed thrasher before it flees again into the shrubbery. Thrashers prefer to scurry into cover instead of flying when threatened—their wings are short and rounded, and they are not particularly good fliers. The California thrasher's bill is quite long, heavy, and down-curved, and the bird uses it like a hoe to rake through leaf litter and loose soil seeking beetles, grubs, and all manner of insects and spiders. It also eats seeds and berries and the fruits of some cacti.

Despite their Wicked-Witch-of-the-West appearance, thrashers are remarkably good singers and accomplished mimics, like their cousin the mockingbird. Adopting a song perch atop a shrub, the thrasher sings for long periods, offering an opportunity to get a good look at this quite common but fairly shy bird.

Thrashers build a bowl-shaped nest of sticks and roots that is hidden among the branches of a shrub. The adult approaches the nest on foot, then hops up to it through the shrub, branch to branch. Most songbird fledglings take flight when they leave the nest, but thrasher young head to the ground. They may spend several days walking, scurrying, and climbing among the shrubs before they test their wings.

When and Where to See Them: Year-round in chaparral, coastal sage scrub, and other dense brushlands in the western half of the state, mainly in central and southern California.

California Thrasher at nest with young

PHAINOPEPLA

Phainopepla nitens
Family: Silky flycatchers
A.K.A.: black flycatcher, shining fly-snapper

Eye-catchers: The handsome phainopepla is known by its black robe, raggedy topknot, bold red eye, and its perch atop a mesquite tree.

The male is silky black with a white wing patch that flashes in flight. The female is gray. Both have startling red eyes, a long tail, and a shaggy crest.

Natural History: Surely this bird's name is a joke, many people think on first seeing it in print. Actually, the phainopepla—pronounced *FAY no PEP la*—just happens to be one of the few birds whose common name is its scientific name. While most birds are christened with a common name that describes it, like the black-capped chickadee, the phainopepla's name is Greek for "shining robe," a charming description of the male's glossy black plumage. Phainopeplas are handsome, slender, and elegant birds, with red eyes that are startling in color and intensity. When the male flies, he flashes bright white wing patches in sharp contrast to his coal black plumage.

While phainopeplas are easy to see, often perching atop a mesquite or other shrub, any close approach will cause them to swoop away to a new perch with a startled whistle or *quirt* call.

The phainopepla's favorite food is the berry of the mistletoe, a parasitic plant that grows in the branches of mesquite and other trees. Old nest sites are often marked by a new growth of mistletoe germinated from seeds left in the nest. Watching phainopeplas feed on mistletoe is quite a sight. They may perch on the plant or hover on the wing, plucking berries like an ancient Greek eating grapes at a bacchanal. They also eat insects, looping out to snag them in flight.

Phainopeplas are not restricted to desert habitats and in California are also found in chaparral and oak woodlands.

When and Where to See Them: Year-round in eastern and southeastern deserts along washes and ravines with small trees.

Phainopepla males

Phainopepla female

LOGGERHEAD SHRIKE

Lanius ludovicianus
Family: Shrikes
A.K.A.: butcher bird, cotton-picker, nine-killer

Eye-catchers: The shrike's black bandit mask, hooked bill, and flashing white wing patches are giveaways.

This stocky bird is dove gray on its back with a white breast and belly and black tail with white outer feathers. A black mask covers the eyes. The bill is sharply hooked, and in flight the black wings flash a white patch.

Natural History: Shrikes are in a class by themselves, songbirds that are fierce predators and act at times like raptors. They are the only songbirds that consistently hunt vertebrate prey, including mice, small birds, and small amphibians and reptiles. They also eat insects. Shrikes don't have the killing talons of birds of prey, but their feet are quite strong for a songbird, with sharp claws. Shrikes have developed a sharp, hooked bill with which they grab and dispatch their prey, delivering a killing bite to the neck. Shrikes may pursue birds in flight, striking them with their bill or sometimes grabbing with their feet and wrestling the prey to the ground. They also hover and drop on prey on the ground. Nicknamed "butcher birds," they commonly impale their prey on a thorn or the barb of a fence until they can return to feed. Shrikes apparently have an astute memory for the places they have cached food. Observers in Texas noted a shrike returned to a desiccated frog eight months after killing it.

The shrike's vision is also remarkable, like that of raptors. Studies found a shrike would fly directly from a treetop perch 600 feet to a trap baited with a live mouse. Another shrike spotted a flying bee at 300 feet, flew directly to it, and plucked it from the air.

In flight, shrikes are remarkably similar to mockingbirds. Both are gray and white with long tails and prominent white wing patches. To tell the two apart, look closely at the body shape and the bill. The shrike's head is much more round, its body more stout, and its bill is hooked like an owl's.

Loggerhead shrikes are very intolerant of human activity and will withdraw from an area if disturbed. Their numbers have decreased over much of their range with increased human development.

When and Where to See Them: Year-round through much of the state in broken woodlands, desert scrub and oases, piñon-juniper woodlands, farms, and sparsely populated suburban areas.

Loggerhead Shrike

SPOTTED TOWHEE

Pipilo maculatus
Family: Sparrows
A.K.A.: ground robin, bush bird, chewink

Eye-catchers: The towhee's handsome red, white, and black plumage and its habit of rustling in the underbrush identify it.

This handsome bird looks a bit like an anorexic robin. It has a black head, breast, and wings, with white spots on its back and wings, red sides, red eyes, and a very long tail.

Natural History: While many members of the sparrow family are a drab brown, the spotted towhee is boldly outfitted in black, white, and red. Not only the towhee's appearance but its behavior draw attention. Towhees are scufflers. They noisily and vigorously shuffle their feet in leaf litter and undergrowth, kicking aside the detritus seeking beetles, moths, caterpillars, seeds, spiders, even small lizards.

The spotted towhee's song is an abbreviated version of the eastern towhee's classic *drink your teeeee*. If towhees are in the neighborhood, you will soon know it. They are ready singers, their churring calls sounding across the scrub even when the birds are invisible. Often, though, a singer takes a song perch atop a shrub, making a colorful, musical sight against the sky. Two males may engage in singing duets. The towhee's call note, sometimes described as *chewink*, also sounds constantly in towhee territory. By contrast, when the female is laying eggs and incubating, she becomes quite secretive and the male rarely comes near the nest. After the young hatch, he helps out in feeding them.

The spotted towhee was formerly known as the rufous-sided towhee, but that designation has been split into two species, the spotted towhee of the West and the eastern towhee of the eastern United States. Another common and easily seen bird, the **California towhee**, is a nondescript brown with a long tail. It was formerly known as the brown towhee.

When and Where to See Them: Year-round in chaparral, dense shrublands, thickets along waterways, wooded canyons, and suburban parks and gardens through much of the state.

Spotted Towhee male

California Towhee

WHITE-CROWNED SPARROW

Zonotrichia leucophrys

Family: Sparrows

A.K.A.: white-crown, Gambel's sparrow

Eye-catchers: Watch for the bold white stripes on the head of this sparrow.

This gray brown sparrow has a pinkish bill and black head boldly striped in white.

Natural History: Sparrows as a group are generally unremarkable birds, lacking in bright colors and showy plumage. The white-crowned sparrow fits this category except in its headgear. The white-crown's black helmet boldly striped with white is quite striking and makes the bird easy to identify. Watch how it erects its head feathers into a slight crest. Researchers have found that the status of a male white-crown is tied to the brightness of his white head stripes. Birds with bright white stripes are dominant and have higher status while lower-status birds, including juveniles, have duller stripes. When researchers painted the head stripes of low-status birds to make them bright, their status in the community went up.

In winter, white-crowned sparrows visit California in great numbers, gathering in feeding flocks in thickets and suburban landscaping. Unlike many birds, white-crowns sing even in winter, their song a joyful trill. The white-crown always gives itself away with its call note, a pert *jip* sounded repeatedly while feeding. Most of the white-crowns in our state are winter visitors, but some live year-round along the coast while others nest in the mountains in summer.

White-crowns forage on the ground for seeds and insects. Using both feet, they scratch backward with a little hop, moving the leaf litter to search for tidbits. They will visit feeders in winter, picking up seed spilled on the ground or using platform feeders set low to the ground.

When and Where to See Them: From mid-September to mid-April in suburban parks, yards, and gardens; thickets and woodlands near water; chaparral; and agricultural land. Some nest in summer along the coast and in mountain meadows and willow thickets.

White-crowned Sparrow

WESTERN MEADOWLARK
Sturnella neglecta
Family: Blackbirds

Eye-catchers: The meadowlark's flutelike song, floating across open country like musical sunshine, is its signature. Watch for the black V against the yellow breast and the flash of white tail edges when the meadowlark flies.

The meadowlark has a streaky gray back and a bright yellow breast marked by a black V-shaped collar.

Natural History: Across the grasslands and open country of the West, the voice of the meadowlark dances like notes from some happy flute. When spring begins to warm California's grasslands, the male meadowlark feels the urge to sing. He has kept quiet all winter but now flies up from his hiding place in the grass to a perch atop a fence post or tall weed. Throwing back his head to expose the bold black chevron gleaming on his butter yellow breast, the bird opens his bill wide. Out tumble the musical notes of his song, as airy and open as the wide sky. Settlers of the nation's prairies welcomed the meadowlark and its cheery song, hearing in the bubbling notes various phrases such as *gee-whiz whillikers, Methodist PREA-cher,* and *oh, yes, I am a pretty-little-bird.*

Flushed into flight, the meadowlark is an easy bird to identify. Its profile shows not much neck, a stubby body, short tail, and short wings beating in a flutter-glide pattern. A sure giveaway is the flash of the white outer tail feathers.

Meadowlarks are cousins to the blackbirds and orioles. Though those birds are known for ganging together in large groups, or troupes, meadowlarks are less social. In summer a field may be full of meadowlarks, but each defends its own nesting territory. Later, family groups of meadowlarks forage together. They may sometimes gather in larger feeding flocks that include northern birds moved south into California for winter.

Meadowlarks build a domed nest of grasses, hidden on the ground beneath a shrub or grass clump, often interwoven with the vegetation. A side entrance allows the adult bird to enter unobtrusively. Meadowlarks are insect eaters, feeding on the grasshoppers, beetles, weevils, and various other insects so abundant in their grassland and open country habitat.

When and Where to See Them: Year-round in grasslands, agricultural lands, and open country through much of the state. They withdraw from cold northern areas in winter.

Western Meadowlark

GREAT-TAILED GRACKLE

Quiscalus mexicanus
Family: Blackbirds
A.K.A.: jackdaw, crow blackbird

Eye-catchers: You'll know this bird by its glossy black plumage, long wedge-shaped tail, and amazing repertoire of vocal sounds (we won't call those raucous noises "songs").

The male grackle is large and very black, his iridescent plumage greenish purple in the sun. His tail is as long as his body and wedge-shaped, the bill long and prominent, and the eyes a startling yellow. The female is bronze brown with paler underparts, dark eyes, and a shorter tail.

Natural History: To be treated to a grackle serenade is a memorable experience, not for its melodious nature but for the amazing cacophony of squawks, shrieks, grunts, and groans these birds can produce. Imagine the shriek of metal on metal, the crumpling of tinfoil, the squawk of chickens, the buzz of a kazoo, and the squeal of brakes, and you have an idea of what a grackle symphony sounds like. Even if the grackle's strident performance hits you like fingernails on a blackboard (a good analogy), the male's regal appearance is impressive. Cloaked in coal black, with a bold, staring eye of yellow, he carries his great tail behind him like the trailing robe of a sultan, stepping with haughty assurance.

Male grackles set up territories, then attract females to them for mating. The male lures in prospective mates with his alluring "song" as he fluffs up his feathers, spreads his wings and fine tail, and vibrates his feathers, striking a pose with bill pointed skyward. He may mate with more than one female in a season, leaving them to attend to all nest chores and rearing of the young. The females build nests amid colonies that can number in the thousands. The female birds squabble over nest sites, pirating nesting material from each other.

Great-tailed grackles were unknown in California until 1964, when one was spotted in Imperial County. They have continued to spread through southeastern California along the Colorado River. In recent years they have begun to show up as far away as the coast and Death Valley and are frequent visitors to the Salton Sea.

When and Where to See Them: Year-round along the Colorado River and in other areas of southern California in agricultural lands, freshwater marshes, and the edges of ponds, lakes, and waterways, expanding into the Central Valley.

Great-tailed Grackle male

Great-tailed Grackle female

SCOTT'S ORIOLE

Icterus parisorum
Family: Blackbirds

Eye-catchers: The black hood spreading down to midbreast, contrasting with butter yellow underparts, distinguishes the Scott's oriole from other orioles.

This oriole has a black head, back, and upper breast and a bright yellow lower breast, belly, and rump. The wings bear white bars and a yellow patch.

Natural History: Orioles are a bright and beautiful group of birds, coming in varying combinations and patterns of black offset by yellow or orange. In the dry scrublands of southern California, the Scott's oriole makes its home, wearing a full cowl of black covering the head and upper breast. Another desert-dwelling oriole, the **hooded oriole,** has a yellow hood with black throat and face. Sometimes called palm orioles, hooded orioles inhabit desert oases and are expanding their range with the spread of palm trees in suburban landscaping.

Scott's orioles are summertime Californians, returning to warmer haunts in Mexico for winter. The male is quite a songster, his clear, whistled song often heard from dawn to dusk. Little is known of the courtship of these desert birds. The males return from Mexico about a week before the females, spending their time clambering determinedly among the tree limbs foraging for insects, all the while singing joyfully. Though the birds themselves may be hard to spot, the trees they inhabit are rocking with song. After mating, the female suspends her complex woven nest of grass and yucca fibers from the outer leaves of yuccas, Joshua trees, or piñon pines. She incubates the eggs, but both parents feed the hatchlings.

Orioles forage for insects, grubs, and other food among the foliage of trees and shrubs and on the ground. They will come to hummingbird feeders for nectar and also to cut fruit, particularly citrus, left out for them.

When and Where to See Them: Late March to mid-August at desert oases and woodlands of Joshua trees and piñon-juniper in southeastern California. Some spend the winter in the lower desert areas of southeastern California.

Scott's Oriole male

Scott's Oriole female

Hooded Oriole male

HOUSE FINCH

Carpodacus mexicanus
Family: Finches
A.K.A.: redhead, rose-breasted house finch, Mexican finch

Eye-catchers: The bright, rosy red head and throat of the male, sometimes appearing orange or even yellow, are an eye-catching contrast to the drab brown of the rest of his plumage.

The male house finch is grayish brown with a rosy red cap, throat, and rump. The female is a streaky grayish brown.

Natural History: Any dedicated feeder of wild birds knows the house finch, one of the most common and abundant feeder birds in the West. So adapted are they to life around humans and the handouts we provide, that these little birds truly are birds of the house.

The house finch range map reveals two broadly separated populations, one in the Southwest and West and the second along the East Coast and into the Midwest. In the 1940s, house finches, native to the Southwest, were collected and sold on the East Coast as caged birds. These "Hollywood finches" were brightly colored and adaptable, but their capture and sale were illegal under the Migratory Bird Treaty. Faced with raids from the authorities, several pet shops in New York City released birds into the wild. Adaptable and hardy, house finches were soon showing up all along the East Coast and expanding inland. Now house finches are well established in their eastern digs, and in places their western and eastern ranges are separated by only 100 miles.

While not a spectacular bird, the house finch is always a pleasing visitor to the backyard, groups of them dotting the shrubbery like a collection of red ornaments on a Christmas tree. The song of the house finch is also pleasant, a bright, flutey collection of notes often ending with a down-slurred *jeeer*.

When and Where to See Them: Year-round through much of the state in open woodlands, riparian areas, agricultural lands, and parks, yards, and gardens in urban, suburban, and town settings.

House Finch male

House Finch female

Mt. Shastina in Siskiyou County

Angeles National Forest

BIRDS OF THE HIGH COUNTRY
Mountains, Canyons, and Forests

Golden Eagle
Peregrine Falcon
Mountain Quail
White-throated Swift/
    Violet-green Swallow
Calliope Hummingbird/
    Rufous Hummingbird
Acorn Woodpecker/
    White-headed Woodpecker
Red-breasted Sapsucker
Northern Flicker/
    Nuttall's Woodpecker
Vermilion Flycatcher
Cliff Swallow
Steller's Jay/
    Western Scrub-Jay
Clark's Nutcracker
Common Raven

Mountain Chickadee
Oak Titmouse
Pygmy Nuthatch/
    White-breasted Nuthatch
Brown Creeper
Canyon Wren
American Dipper
Western Bluebird
Mountain Bluebird
American Robin
Varied Thrush/Hermit Thrush
Western Tanager/
    Summer Tanager
Wilson's Warbler/
    Townsend's Warbler
Black-headed Grosbeak
Dark-eyed Junco
Red Crossbill

GOLDEN EAGLE

Aquila chrysaetos

Family: Hawks and eagles

A.K.A.: mountain eagle, royal eagle, king of birds, American war eagle

Eye-catchers: The golden eagle's large size and all-brown plumage, as well as its very broad wingspan, distinguish it from hawks.

Significantly larger than a hawk, the golden eagle is a rich brown with a lighter golden wash over its head and nape. Its legs are feathered down to the feet. Immature birds have a white tail with a dark terminal band.

Natural History: Found throughout the Northern Hemisphere, the golden eagle has been a symbol of power and majesty to many cultures though the centuries. Native Americans prized their feathers as tokens of strength and valor. In Europe only royalty were permitted to use eagles for falconry, and eagles appear on heraldic symbols and crests of arms of European royal families. Today we still regard the eagle as the epitome of freedom and untamed strength, and the sight of one soaring always stirs the spirit.

While the bald eagle lives near water, the golden eagle is a bird of rugged cliffs, canyons, and nearby open country. Golden eagles mate for life, the pair building a large stick nest on an inaccessible cliff overlooking open country. The golden eagle feeds on a broad range of birds, reptiles, and mammals, as well as carrion. The eagle's legendary ability to carry off calves and lambs, and in some fairy tales young children, is just that—a legend. Studies found that an adult golden eagle weighing 11 pounds could comfortably carry 2 pounds of weight, but could not lift off if 5-pound weights were attached to its feet. Adult male eagles weigh 11 to 13 pounds and females 15 to 20 pounds. In the past golden eagles were killed in great numbers for recreation and by ranchers who feared they preyed on livestock. Golden eagles are now protected under federal law.

The largest of North American raptors, the golden eagle is a powerful hunter, soaring on its wide wings for hours. Spotting prey on the ground, the eagle thunders earthward in an immense "stoop" or predatory dive, reaching speeds estimated at up to 200 miles per hour, then grabbing and killing its prey in sharp, powerful talons.

When and Where to See Them: Throughout the state in summer in cliff habitat or areas of tall trees bordering on open country, expanding into open woodlands, grasslands, agricultural land, desert edges, and valleys the rest of the year.

Golden Eagle

PEREGRINE FALCON

Falco peregrinus
Family: Falcons
A.K.A.: duck hawk, wandering falcon, rock peregrine

Eye-catchers: The peregrine's flight profile is classically falconlike, long wings tapering to points, long tail, and slender streamlined body. Up close, look for the single cheek "whisker."

This slender, medium-sized raptor has a deep slate blue back and wings and pale undersides with dark barring. The head has a blue helmet with a wide bar or "whisker" on the cheek. The tail is long and the wings are tapered and pointed.

Natural History: The peregrine falcon became synonymous not just with the serious decline of wildlife species but with the loss of American wilderness. By the early 1970s this magnificent blue falcon had disappeared from most of its range in the lower 48 states, the victim of liberal use of DDT and other pesticides. These poisons concentrated through the food chain, and top-level predators like peregrines and bald eagles suffered the effects—producing eggs with egg-shells too thin and fragile to survive. A recovery effort by biologists nationwide included removing eggs from wild nests for safe hatching in laboratories, and later placing the resultant chicks back in their parents' nests. Imagine the commitment of biologists who scaled cliffs to reach the wild aeries, risking the wrath of the adult falcons to install those fragile chicks in cliff-top nests. By 1994 the peregrine was sufficiently recovered for one subspecies to be removed from the endangered species list.

In California, peregrines are seen not only on mountains but often hunting over ponds and wetlands. Their preference for eating waterfowl and haunting wildfowl preserves in hunting season seeking cripples led to their previous common name, duck hawk. But the classic peregrine hunting scenario takes place in a steep-walled canyon, where the arrow-winged falcon stoops on prey in a high-speed dive. Circling among the canyon walls, the peregrine spots a flicker, pigeon, or other bird flying below. The falcon suddenly plummets at up to 275 miles per hour, slashing with its open talons, then dropping to grab the dead bird from the air or recovering it on the ground.

When and Where to See Them: Statewide in spring and summer along sea cliffs and inland cliffs and canyons near interior lakes. Mid-September to mid-May the length of the state primarily west of the Sierra Nevada, occasionally inhabiting skyscrapers in downtown Los Angeles.

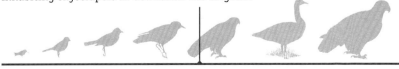

Peregrine Falcon

Peregrine Falcon in flight

MOUNTAIN QUAIL

Oreortyx pictus
Family: New World quail
A.K.A.: painted quail, plumed quail, mountain partridge

Eye-catchers: The arrow-straight feathers projecting pertly from the bird's head differentiates it from other quail.

This large, gray brown quail has chestnut sides with white stripes and two long, straight feather plumes on its head. The female is duller, with shorter plumes.

Natural History: With its upright head plumes, which stick straight up when the bird is alarmed or curious, the mountain quail seems to wear a perpetual look of surprise. Rely upon this straight headdress to tell the mountain quail from the similar California quail, whose plume curls forward and is plumper at the tip.

Mountain quail inhabit dense brushy and forested areas in the mountains, also moving into open mountain meadows seeking food. Mountain quail feed on buds, seeds, nuts, fruit, and flowers. They migrate up and down the mountainsides with the seasons, following the bloom and the fruit and berry crops. This may entail moves of 30 miles, which might not seem like much for a bird, considering some birds migrate 5,000 miles. But the ground-dwelling quail doesn't fly the distance, it walks, moving through the underbrush with its chickenlike, head-thrusting gait. Like other ground-dwelling grouse and pheasants, quail generally take wing only for short distances, usually when fleeing a predator. Anyone who has ever been surprised by a covey of quail exploding practically underfoot recognizes the effectiveness of a sudden and startling escape strategy for confusing the enemy. Once flushed, the covey flies only a short distance, landing to scurry away on foot into the dense brush.

In spring, males choose a spot atop a rock or bush and begin a whistling song. Once paired with a mate, the two separate from the covey and build a concealed nest at the base of a tree or log, lining it with grass, feathers, and pine needles. The young are able to follow their parents soon after hatching. The sight of a quail family, two plump adults followed by a line of puffball babies, is charming.

When and Where to See Them: Year-round in upper-elevation desert scrub and in foothill and mountain forests through much of the state.

Mountain Quail male

WHITE-THROATED SWIFT

Aeronautes saxatalis
Family: Swifts
A.K.A.: rock swift, canyon swift

Eye-catchers: The swift's scimitar wings and black-and-white patterned underside identify it.

This swift is black with a white throat, a broad white stripe down the breast and belly, and white patches along the sides at the rear that contrast with dark patches under the wings. It has very long, slender wings.

Natural History: This swift is one bird you can bet money you will see only in flight. Swifts are birds of the air, their feet so tiny and weak that they cannot perch well, and to take off they must fall into the air from a cliff-edge perch. This family's Latin name, Apodidae, means "without feet." But who needs feet when you can fly like this? On the wing, swifts are aerial poetry. Their long, slender wings cut the air like knives, carrying them swooping between canyon walls like stunt jets. In the airspace above a steep-walled canyon swifts flash back and forth, arcing and diving with speed and grace. Their charming calls seem to reflect their joy in flight, a laughing chatter that echoes off the rocks.

Swifts are thought to be the fastest-flying birds; they have been observed eluding the stoop of a peregrine falcon estimated at more than 200 miles per hour. They hunt on the wing like swallows, snapping insects from the air. Their mouths, opening literally ear to ear, spread in a wide gape to help them scoop up flying prey. They also court and mate on the wing, the mating pair tumbling together hundreds of feet before taking wing again. The adults construct a nest of grass and feathers cemented with their saliva into a crevice on a cliff accessible only by air, keeping their young very safe from predators.

Though they resemble swallows, swifts are not closely related to them at all. Swifts are not even songbirds; oddly enough, they are cousins to hummingbirds. White-throated swifts can be differentiated from **violet-green swallows,** which share their canyon habitat, by the pattern of black and white on the swift's underside; the swallow is all white underneath.

When and Where to See Them: Year-round in central coastal mountains and through much of southern California in areas of cliffs, bluffs, and steep canyons. In summer also in more northern mountains. Also in cities, where they often nest in crevices of freeway structures.

White-throated Swift

Violet-green Swallow male

CALLIOPE HUMMINGBIRD
Stellula calliope
Family: Hummingbirds

Eye-catchers: The calliope's tiny size—it is a peewee even in a family of midgets—and its streaky purple throat are its signature.

This emerald green hummingbird is pale below with purple streaking on its pale throat, with some of the purple feathers projecting beyond the throat like whiskers. The bill is needlelike. The female is green above, pale below, with a buffy wash across the breast and under the wings.

Natural History: In a family of tiny birds, the calliope is the tiniest, measuring only $2^{3}/_{4}$ to $3^{1}/_{2}$ inches long, and that includes the bill! Calliope hummingbirds are the smallest birds in North America north of Mexico, weighing only $^{1}/_{10}$ of an ounce. Yet they are Herculean in strength for their size. A male calliope was observed lifting a female hummingbird that had flown into a window. He grasped her bill in his and fluttered with his burden to a height of 3 feet before losing his grip. The male lifted and lost the female several more times. Luckily the story ends happily; the observer warmed the female in his hands until she revived and flew off.

The calliope's Latin name translates to something like "pleasant-voiced little star." This tiny hummer is the namesake of Calliope, one of the Muses of Greek mythology. Perhaps this comes from the impressive courtship flights the male performs. Winging perhaps 100 feet in the air, the tiny bird zings earthward, a shrill green bullet, pulling up with a buzz at the bottom of his dive right in front of the female.

In California, calliope hummers brighten up mountain meadows and open forests with their buzzing flight and bright flashes of iridescent emerald. Hummingbirds as a family are birds of the tropics, but the calliope moves quite far north and up in altitude, sometimes nesting above 10,000 feet in the Sierra Nevada. Male hummers survive the cold nights by gearing down their metabolisms and entering a nightly torpor.

In spring the **rufous hummingbird** moves northward up the Pacific Coast, a few remaining to nest in northwestern California. Bright as a copper penny, the rufous is the most aggressive of hummingbirds, frequently taking over feeders and flower beds from more docile species.

When and Where to See Them: Early April through September mainly in northern and central California in mountain forests, mountain meadows, shrub thickets near water, and hillsides with flowering shrubs and wildflowers.

Calliope Hummingbird male

Rufous Hummingbird male

ACORN WOODPECKER

Melanerpes formicivorus
Family: Woodpeckers
A.K.A.: ant-eating woodpecker

Eye-catchers: Dressed like a harlequin in bold black, white, and red plumage with a prominent yellow eye, the acorn woodpecker stands out.

This black woodpecker has a bright red cap, its head boldly marked in contrasting patches of black and white. Its underparts are a streaky white, and it has a white rump and wing patches. The bold yellow eye is quite prominent.

Natural History: Subtlety, either in dress or behavior, is not the stock-in-trade of the acorn woodpecker. Visit its forest habitat and you can't miss these large, black woodpeckers, their caps flashing a bright red, their faces a clown's mask of black and white with a staring yellow eye. Acorn woodpeckers are ever busy, flying from one tree to the next, gathering acorns and caching them for future use. Watch closely and you'll see the birds fly a circuit, returning to the same trees with acorns or other booty. You can't miss their loud, characteristic call, described as *JA-cob* or *WAKE-up*. Listen carefully for their tap-tap-tapping as they wedge acorns into holes they've drilled in the bark of their storehouse trees, for rather than pecking into bark for insects as their prime food source, acorn woodpeckers gather acorns and other nuts and cache them. The trunks of some large trees are pockmarked with hundreds of stored acorns.

Acorn woodpeckers live in colonies of from 2 to 15 birds, often extended families of a breeding pair and their offspring. The colony can harvest and store a vast amount of food, providing them a food source for the winter. These woodpeckers guard their storehouse well, attacking squirrels and other birds that attempt a raid. The extended family also shares in rearing the young, taking turns incubating the eggs and feeding the nestlings. Acorn woodpecker reproduction is tied to the crop of its primary food; in a poor acorn year a pair produces few offspring, while in an abundant year they may raise a large family.

Another seed-eating woodpecker of the California hills, forests, and mountains is the **white-headed woodpecker,** which feeds on pine nuts. This black woodpecker has a white face, throat, and breast (the male has a red spot on the nape). It is the only white-headed woodpecker in North America.

When and Where to See Them: Year-round throughout most of the state in oak woodlands, sycamore forests, and mixed oak-conifer forests.

Acorn Woodpecker male

Storehouse of an Acorn Woodpecker

White-headed Woodpecker male

RED-BREASTED SAPSUCKER

Sphyrapicus ruber
Family: Woodpeckers
A.K.A.: yellow-bellied sapsucker

Eye-catchers: The reddish head and breast in counterpoint to its white-speckled black back and yellowish belly identify this sapsucker.

This black-backed woodpecker has a red head and breast and pale speckles on the sides. In flight it flashes a white rump and white shoulder patches.

Natural History: Part of the genus name for sapsuckers, *sphyra,* means "hammer," an appropriate reference for a bird that pecks into tree bark with its hammering bill. Sapsuckers have an interesting mode of feeding. They drill a series of holes into the trunk of a tree, then consume the sap that fills in these "wells." In the process they also get protein by eating insects that become trapped in the sap. Other birds, particularly hummingbirds, also drink the tree sap, and sapsucker wells are likely an important food source for hummingbirds when flowers are not yet in full bloom.

Like many specialized families of birds, woodpeckers have evolved numerous physical tools and adaptations, in this case for the job of pecking wood. Their feet are designed for clinging to the side of a tree. The first and fourth toes point backward and the middle two toes forward, creating a sort of X pattern that gives them not only a good grip on the tree but better stability for hammering. The two central tail feathers are quite stiff to help brace the bird against the trunk. The bill is strong, hard, and straight, an effective chisel. To absorb the shock of pecking wood, the skull is thick-walled, the head muscles strong, and there is a cushioning space between the brain and its outer membrane.

While other birds serenade prospective mates with melodious song, woodpeckers tap out their message of courtship. Finding a particularly resonant drum—perhaps a dead tree or sometimes the side of a house—the male woodpecker adopts it as his drumming post much like a courting songbird does a song perch. The characteristic tattoo of the red-breasted sapsucker is a burst of taps followed by several irregular beats. The male and female red-breasted sapsucker are alike in appearance, rare among woodpeckers.

When and Where to See Them: Spring through fall in moist, coastal coniferous forests and mixed forests of interior mountains, in winter moving to lower elevations and more diverse woodlands in the southern part of the state.

Red-breasted Sapsucker at sap well on aspen tree

Sapsucker drillings

NORTHERN FLICKER

Colaptes auratus
Family: Woodpeckers
A.K.A.: wake-up, harrywicket, red-shafted flicker

Eye-catchers: Watch for the bold white flash of the flicker's rump and its reddish wings in flight. The flicker's loud, nasal call also betrays its presence.

The backs of these large, brown woodpeckers are speckled with black. They have a black crescent on the chest, and the male has a bright red "mustache" on each cheek. In flight the flicker flashes a white rump and rusty red wing linings and tail.

Natural History: Flickers are perhaps the most familiar and ubiquitous of woodpeckers, comfortable as they are with setting up housekeeping around people. As common in cities, parks, and yards as they are in the woods, flickers are noisy and showy, poking on the ground for ants, drilling into trees after insects, and flying from tree to tree with a dipping, undulating flight. Their loud *yuk yuk yuk* call, sounding in an open woodland or a suburban neighborhood, boldly tells us a flicker is in residence.

With its long sturdy bill, muscular neck, and body braced vertically on a tree trunk, the flicker, like all woodpeckers, is designed to drill wood. Interestingly, foraging for insects in tree bark is not the flicker's main mode of finding food. Flickers spend much more time on the ground than most woodpeckers, feeding on insects, particularly ants, which make up nearly half of their diet. The flicker's typical woodpecker tongue is very long, some 3 inches. With its brushy tongue tip and sticky saliva, the flicker sweeps up ants like a housekeeper dusting with an oily dust rag.

Flickers hollow out nest cavities in trees that in subsequent years provide holes for smaller species such as chickadees and swallows, which need cavities to protect their nests but whose bills are not designed for such heavy excavation work.

Nuttall's woodpecker, with a back barred in black and white, spotted sides, and a red nape on the male, makes its home in chaparral and streamside woodlands. While the northern flicker is found throughout North America, Nuttall's woodpecker lives primarily in California west of the Sierra Nevada, with some overlap of its range into neighboring states.

When and Where to See Them: Year-round through much of the state in riparian and mixed coniferous-deciduous woodlands, agricultural tree stands, and urban and suburban yards, parks, and gardens.

Northern Flicker male with young in nesting hole

Nuttall's Woodpecker male on underside of branch

VERMILION FLYCATCHER

Pyrocephalus rubinus
Family: Tyrant flycatchers
A.K.A.: redbird

Eye-catchers: A flash of brilliant red in the trees signals the vermilion flycatcher.

The male has a dark brown back, brilliant red head and underparts, a brown eye mask, and a head crest that it raises when aroused. The female is brown with a streaked breast and salmon belly.

Natural History: "Fire head" is the translation for the vermilion flycatcher's genus name—*Pyrocephalus*—and an apt description of this brilliantly colored bird. In Mexico it is known as *sangre de toro,* or the "blood of the bull."

With its bold costume, the vermilion is an exception in the flycatcher family. Most of its cousins are a drab gray, with a few showing washes of yellow. The vermilion flycatcher stands out not only for its appearance but for its behavior. During spring courtship the male puts on quite a show for the female. With jaunty crest upraised and tail fanned he rises into the air, singing a tinkling melody. He pauses and hovers like a butterfly on rapidly beating wings, then rises farther, alternating hovering and fluttering until he reaches a height of as much as 50 feet. Then he slowly flutters down in front of his female audience, who, one hopes, is suitably impressed.

The mated pair chooses a nest site in the crotch of a cottonwood or other tree near water, building a sturdy saucer-shaped nest of twigs lined with plant down and animal hair. The male flycatcher is a dutiful mate. As the female incubates her eggs, he feeds her and keeps a protective watch over the home.

In California, vermilion flycatchers enliven wooded thickets of southeastern desert oases. These busy scraps of red bring color to the desert landscape, flitting out to catch insects in flight, then circling back to their perches. If vegetation is dense, they may be hard to see because they inhabit the upper branches, but in sparser cover they are easier to spot, especially when they land on the ground to catch grasshoppers. Vermilion flycatchers are particularly adept at catching bees in flight.

When and Where to See Them: In lowland desert oases vegetated with shrubs and trees, mid-March through April, in southern and southeastern California.

Vermilion Flycatcher male

CLIFF SWALLOW

Petrochelidon pyrrhonota
Family: Swallows
A.K.A.: mud swallow, crescent swallow, Capistrano swallow

Eye-catchers: In flight, watch for the cliff swallow's red-and-white face and pale belly. Watch also for the gourd-shaped mud nests of cliff swallows glued beneath an overhang or bridge.

This blue-black swallow has a pale belly, rusty red face and rump, and a white crescent on the forehead. The tail is square, not swallow-tailed.

Natural History: The cliff swallow is the legendary swallow of the Mission San Juan Capistrano. Since 1777, the swallows have reputedly returned faithfully to the mission every March 19 to nest beneath its eaves and arches. But as with all legends, this one needs a little wiggle room. Though swallows have returned there year after year, the date of return varies slightly, depending on weather and seasonal conditions. The swallows are charming summer residents of the old mission, although their numbers are declining due to urbanization of the area.

The sight of dozens of cliff swallows swirling in the air beneath a bridge, all diving and swooping with nary a collision, is enthralling. Slender and sleek, with long pointed wings, swallows are marvelous aerialists. Their primary feathers, the "fingertips" of the wings, are up to twice as long as the secondary feathers—those on the wing's long, trailing edge—allowing the wing to cut and slice through the air for tight maneuvers. With its wide mouth gaping open, the swallow engulfs flying insects, helped along by bristles around the mouth that act like a catcher's mitt to scoop up prey.

Cliff swallows build nests of mud glued beneath bridges, rock overhangs, the eaves of buildings, and other protected spots. The adults make dozens of visits to a mud hole or streamside, scooping mouthfuls of mud that they plaster, dab after dab, to build the nest. A colony of cliff swallow nests looks like a cluster of gourds glued to a cliff, the round openings appearing like dozens of eyes. With an insect in its bill, the parent swallow zooms in toward its particular nest, seemingly on a collision course, only to pull up in time to pop slickly through the tight opening. After a few moments the adult's head reappears in the hole, then the bird launches out again on the wing.

When and Where to See Them: In southern California beginning in mid-January, spreading through much of the state by April, through late August. Near water at cliffs, bridges, ocean bluffs, dams, mine shafts, and road cuts almost statewide.

A pair of Cliff Swallows building a nest

STELLER'S JAY

Cyanocitta stelleri
Family: Crows
A.K.A.: mountain jay, pine jay, coast jay, black-headed jay

Eye-catchers: A blue bird with a black crest is none other than the Steller's jay. You also cannot miss its harsh *shak shak* call.

This handsome jay is cobalt blue with a black head and crest.

Natural History: Walking in a mountain pine forest, you suddenly hear a harsh, rasping call—*shak shak shak!* Then the caller materializes in a tree above your head, a handsome bird in royal blue with a perky black crest. The Steller's jay is a common resident of coniferous forests. Though bold like most of its cousins in the crow family, the Steller's jay becomes rather shy during nesting season, behaving circumspectly in the vicinity of its nest. But come armed with a picnic basket and the Steller's jays will certainly find you, arriving in hopes of a tidbit. Typically, they land in the lower branches of trees, working their way to the top hopping limb to limb, then flying down into a neighboring tree.

Visitors often mistakenly refer to Steller's jays as blue jays, but this western species is very different in appearance and habitat from its eastern cousin. Despite frequent confusion over its name, this jay is named for a German biologist, Georg Wilhelm Steller, who shot the first specimen along the Alaskan coast during a 1741 expedition. Its name is not from the word *stellar,* which is spelled differently and means "starry" or "outstanding."

Largest among North American jays, the Steller's jay eats mainly pine nuts, which explains its favored habitat, and other plant material, adding protein to its diet with insects and the eggs of other nesting birds. In contrast to its raucous call, the Steller's utters a soft "whisper song" when near the nest, and gives an excellent imitation of the scream of a red-tailed hawk.

Steller's jays do not migrate but may move to lower-elevation woodlands in winter. The **western scrub-jay** is another bright-blue jay inhabiting woodland and lower-elevation mountain habitats and urban neighborhoods. Its undersides are gray and it lacks a crest.

When and Where to See Them: Year-round in mountain and coastal coniferous forests.

Steller's Jay
Western Scrub-Jay

CLARK'S NUTCRACKER

Nucifraga columbiana
Family: Crows
A.K.A.: camp robber, meat hawk, woodpecker crow

Eye-catchers: Watch for the nutcracker's black-and-white wings and tail. Its raucous *kraaow kraaow* call will announce this opportunist's appearance at a mountain picnic.

This large, gray member of the crow and jay family has a long bill and black wings, tail, bill, and legs. The tail is edged in white, and the wings show white patches in flight.

Natural History: The Clark's nutcracker is named for Captain William Clark of the Lewis and Clark expedition, which first recorded this species. The expedition's journals note, "It is about the size and somewhat the form of the Jaybird . . . and has a loud squawling note something like the mewing of a cat." Clark immediately knew this new bird was a member of the crow family, both from its unrefined and raucous voice and its assertive personality. The nutcracker is a boisterous and gregarious bird, living year-round in high mountain forests, where it gathers pine nuts as its primary food. Flocks of as many as 100 birds may gather together to feed in the trees. Nutcrackers have a special pouch beneath their tongue that allows them to carry dozens of pine nuts, which they harvest in summer and fall and cache for winter. Studies show that nutcrackers choose south-facing slopes as their cache sites—north-facing slopes would be deep in snow through winter—finding the buried booty again by memory, often marking the site with twigs or pebbles. Of course, many cached seeds are not found again by the nutcrackers and germinate. Because of their dispersal of seeds, the birds are important in the reproductive cycle of some species of pine.

To open the tough-hulled pine nuts, the nutcracker holds the seed in the toes of one foot and cracks it with its bill. Individual birds are either "left-handed" or "right-handed," consistently favoring the use of one foot for holding seeds. Nutcrackers also eat insects, and their rather uncrowlike habit of clinging to the trunks of trees and pecking at the bark like a woodpecker led to the nickname "woodpecker crow."

When and Where to See Them: Year-round in high-elevation, mountain pine forests through much of the state.

Clark's Nutcracker

COMMON RAVEN

Corvus corax
Family: Crows
A.K.A.: northern raven, American raven

Eye-catchers: This large, black bird haunting cliffs and mountains can be distinguished from the crow by its larger size. Its tail ends in a wedge rather than straight across like a crow's.

This very large, glossy black bird has a long, heavy arched bill and shaggy throat feathers.

Natural History: A black shadow rakes silently across the rocky face of a mountain slope, then skims the grass of a mountain meadow. With effortless grace the raven commands its mountain kingdom, conveying an otherworldly bearing to simple mortals watching from the ground. Few birds figure so greatly in the folklore and mythology of human cultures worldwide as the raven. Found not only in North America but in northern Europe, Asia, and Africa, the raven is variably considered a wise ancient one, a messenger from the gods, a soothsayer, and a harbinger of evil. Ravens figure in Native American mythology of tribes throughout the West as creator, ancestor, or trickster. In the Bible, Noah sent out a raven to test the floodwaters. And who can forget the sepulchral raven of Edgar Allan Poe's poem that ominously quoth "Nevermore."

Whether or not you consider the raven a supernatural creature, it is a marvelous bird to watch. In spring, male ravens perform a spectacular aerial display, soaring, swooping, and tumbling for their mates in the high airspaces of canyons and mountains. Canyon country can seem filled with raven pairs, their black shapes dancing in the air as their hollow calls echo off the rocks. Some of their playful behavior seems to have no explanation except that—play. Watching them soar, effortless and free, banking around each other like partners in a dance, it seems an apt explanation. One observer reported seeing a raven playing on a snowbank, rolling down the snow like a slide, then walking back to the top and rolling down again, over and over.

When and Where to See Them: Year-round in mountains, deserts, suburbs, and open country statewide.

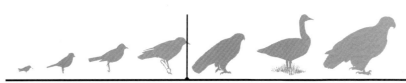

Common Raven

Common Raven in flight (note wedge-shaped tail)

MOUNTAIN CHICKADEE

Poecile gambeli
Family: Titmice
A.K.A.: Inyo chickadee, short-tailed chickadee

Eye-catchers: A white stripe above the eye distinguishes the mountain chickadee from its cousin the black-capped chickadee.

This sprightly little bird has a gray back, pale undersides, black bib and cap, and a white line above the eye.

Natural History: The mountain and black-capped chickadees are sort of like two siblings who are almost similar enough to be twins, but not quite. The distinguishing white line above the eye makes a mountain chickadee stand out. And the mountain's call is more raspy and hoarse than the black-capped's—*tsik a zee zee*—and its song is three-noted—*fee bee bee* instead of *fee bee*—going down with each note. These differences aside, the mountain chickadee conveys the same sprightly energy and sense of goodwill that its family is known for. Confusion between the two species is not much of an issue in California, however, since the black-capped breeds only sparingly in the northwestern part of the state.

True to their name, mountain chickadees live in high mountain forests throughout the year, moving to lower elevations in winter. They comb the bark of pine and other trees for insects, nesting in cavities in trees that have been excavated by woodpeckers. While a chickadee can enlarge or shape an existing cavity, its bill is too weak for the job of excavating an entire new hole.

The mountain chickadee's hallmark, its white eyebrow, wears off throughout the summer. The eyebrow feathers are actually black with white tips. As the adults come and go from the nest cavity, rubbing against the opening, they gradually wear away these tips, until by summer's end the eyebrow is no longer a crisp white but either grizzled or completely worn away. After the fall moult the chickadee wears a fresh coat of eye makeup.

When and Where to See Them: Year-round through much of the state in higher mountain coniferous forests, moving also into lowland woodlands in winter.

Mountain Chickadee

OAK TITMOUSE

Baeolophus inornatus
Family: Titmice
A.K.A.: gray titmouse, San Diego titmouse, plain titmouse

Eye-catchers: The titmouse's crest is the only distinguishing characteristic of this otherwise plain, gray bird.

This tiny gray bird has an upright crest.

Natural History: The oak titmouse was formerly known as the plain titmouse, but it might just as well have been called the plain-Jane titmouse, so unremarkable is it save for its perky head crest, which gives the little bird an inquisitive expression. But plain or not, the titmouse is an endearing bird to watch, endowed with such a degree of energy and industry it puts a honeybee to shame. Titmice always seem to be moving, flitting among the tree branches, hanging upside down like trapeze artists to reach a grub in a particularly inaccessible bark crevice, or poking around on the ground after nuts, seeds, and insects.

Titmice are first cousins to the chickadee, and the family resemblance is evident in the titmouse's *tsik a dee* call. Also like the chickadee, the titmouse builds its nest in a hole in a tree, fence post, or other crevice selected by the female. At the bottom of the nest hole, the adults weave a soft little cup of hair, plant fibers, and down to hold their eggs. The titmouse pair makes a faithful couple; once mated they stay together year after year until one dies. When the female is incubating eggs, the male feeds her, and she flutters her wings and gives a squeaky call as if in thanks (or maybe she's asking for more). Once the young leave the nest, they are driven from their parents' territory to face life on their own.

When and Where to See Them: Year-round in piñon-juniper and mixed oak woodlands through much of the state.

Oak Titmouse

PYGMY NUTHATCH

Sitta pygmaea
Family: Nuthatches
A.K.A.: pine nuthatch, black-eared nuthatch

Eye-catchers: A tiny bird moving headfirst down a tree trunk and looking as if its gray brown cap is pulled down over its eyes is a pygmy nuthatch.

This small nuthatch is blue gray with white underparts and outer tail edges and a gray brown cap that extends down to the eye line. It has a short neck and tail.

Natural History: The first time someone sees a nuthatch, they are always taken aback. As the busy bug-eater works its way headfirst down a tree trunk in a gravity-defying act of avian acrobatics, one can't help but wonder, "How does it do that?" This rather unorthodox mode of finding a meal makes the nuthatch unique. In the animal world, evolving ways to find food that no one else is taking advantage of allows a species competition-free access to a food source. While other birds glean insects from leaves or peck beneath tree bark, only the nuthatches minutely search the tree trunk by moving down the tree, carefully combing for insects hidden in crevices from that specific angle. Pygmy nuthatches forage among the outer branches of trees more than the other nuthatches.

Nuthatches are great fun to watch, busy, quirky, upside-down birds going about their business despite our open-mouthed surprise at their feats. Nuthatches are not svelte birds; their bodies are plump and football-shaped, appearing neckless with a head that slopes from the shoulders into the long, pointed bill. The nuthatch bill is like a fine tweezers, designed for poking into crevices and plucking out tiny critters. For this incredibly close work, the nuthatch is extremely nearsighted, able to focus at a fraction of an inch.

The aptly named pygmy nuthatch is the smallest of the four species of nuthatch in North America. It is a bird of the mountains, preferring ponderosa and other pine forests at high elevations, where it lives year-round, caching pine nuts as winter provender. During the cold months pygmy nuthatches gather in large groups, foraging and roosting together in crevices. One old hollow pine tree was found to shelter some 150 nuthatches, all huddling together like a Brownie troop around the campfire.

The **white-breasted nuthatch,** known by its white cheeks and narrow black panel across the top of its head, prefers lower deciduous forests and woodlands near water.

When and Where to See Them: Year-round in mountain pine forests throughout the state.

Pygmy Nuthatch
White-breasted Nuthatch male

BROWN CREEPER

Certhia americana
Family: Creepers
A.K.A.: California creeper, Sierra creeper, tree creeper

Eye-catchers: A slender, little brown bird moving *up* the trunk of a tree just has to be a creeper.

This slim, brown bird is streaked and speckled with white, with lighter undersides, a long tail, a white line over the eye, and a very long, sharp, down-curving bill.

Natural History: In the bird world, somebody is always coming or going, and while the nuthatches are coming down the tree trunk, the creepers are going *up*. Creepers are not particularly remarkable in appearance, essentially a speckled brown. You might say they look like tree bark (this is not an accident). It's what a creeper does that's interesting. These little birds with bills like long, curving tweezers busily run up the trunks of trees, peering into crevices, poking into notches, turning this way and that, spiraling ever upward as if they are walking up the side of a wall wearing antigravity boots. When it reaches a horizontal limb, the creeper doesn't slow down but continues its search, traveling upside down with its back parallel to the ground. Having reached the top of one thoroughly searched tree, the creeper flies down to the bottom of a neighboring tree to begin the process again.

Creepers have found their niche (both ecologically and literally). By traveling up the trunks of trees, minutely inspecting every crack and crevice, they comb the bark for insects from a different perspective than nuthatches, chickadees, woodpeckers, or other bark-gleaning insect eaters. A grub secreted in a bark crevice at an angle that is hidden from the downward-traveling nuthatch may be visible from the angle of the upwardly mobile creeper.

Creepers are a small family, with only six species worldwide. All are in the Northern Hemisphere, but only our brown creeper lives in North America. In California it dwells year-round in coniferous or mixed-species forests, often moving to lower elevations in winter. You may hear its high-pitched *tsee* call in a dense forest without ever seeing the little brown creeper itself.

When and Where to See Them: Year-round in dense coniferous forests or mixed-species woodlands, in mountains and coastal forests throughout much of the state, moving to lowland valleys and foothills in winter.

Brown Creeper

CANYON WREN

Catherpes mexicanus
Family: Wrens
A.K.A.: bugler, dotted wren

Eye-catchers: The liquid, cascading song of the canyon wren announces its presence.

The canyon wren's plumage is brownish red speckled with white. Its throat and breast are white, with a chestnut belly. The bill is long.

Natural History: You're hiking in a steep, rocky canyon when a marvelous, tinkling melody cascades down the canyon walls like a musical waterfall. The song of the canyon wren is certainly one of the most beautiful and delightful of birdsongs, matching so well the rock-tumbled habitats where this bird makes its home. Even if you never see a canyon wren, and they aren't easy to spot, just hearing its wonderful music, the clear notes cascading down the scale like a ball bouncing down a musical staircase, is enough of a reward.

Actually seeing a canyon wren usually involves patient, cautious stalking, following the wren's song. Even then, spotting the bird against its rocky habitat takes keen eyes, but once located, the bird's white throat bib is like an identifying flag. The canyon wren is typically wrenlike in appearance, with a plump body, short neck, small head, and long slender bill. Its pert tail is less often held up-cocked in classic wren style.

Many of us might think of wrens as birds of marshes and moist woodlands, but the canyon wren is a bird of the cliffs and watered canyons of the West. It putters about over the rocks, poking in, under, and around rocks, cracks, and crevices for insects and spiders. Canyon wrens construct a nest secreted beneath a rock, in a tiny canyon alcove, or on a hidden ledge, first laying a foundation of sticks, then layering it with leaves, spiderwebs, and mosses, finally adding a soft lining of animal fur and feathers. Not a great deal is known about the life history of this charming bird, and it bears further study.

When and Where to See Them: Year-round in steep canyons, cliffs, and rocky outcroppings through much of the state.

Canyon Wren

AMERICAN DIPPER

Cinclus mexicanus
Family: Dippers
A.K.A.: water ouzel

Eye-catchers: A songbird that suddenly jumps into a mountain stream and walks in under the water just has to be a dipper.

This rather nondescript bird is a sooty gray with a short tail and stubby bill.

Natural History: Many species of waterfowl and shorebirds are adapted to life in the air, on land, and in and under the water. But how many songbirds can make this claim? The wonderful and amazing dipper is such a bird, deserving of all the admiring adjectives for its extraordinary lifestyle. Dippers live along rushing mountain streams, jumping under the water to feed on insects, larvae, and other invertebrate prey. Like a scuba diver, the dipper makes use of special equipment. It wears diving goggles—a special third eyelid that closes over the eye to protect it from debris while still allowing the bird to see. It dons a wet suit by coating itself with water-repellent oil—the preen gland of the dipper is 10 times larger than those of other songbirds, and its plumage is especially dense and watertight. It has a watertight hatch—a flap of skin closes over the nostrils to keep out water. It "flies" underwater, using its wings to propel itself through the water.

The dipper isn't much of a bird to look at, resembling a dark gray starling. But keep your eyes peeled and you will see this bird seem to turn into a fish. Standing at the edge of a rushing stream, the dipper suddenly dives into the water, or sometimes wades in, disappearing beneath the surface to walk on the bottom or swim. If you're lucky you may see it break through the surface and fly up out of the water all in one motion, like some fantasy underwater airplane from a James Bond film. Dippers often fly up and down stream courses just above the water, following the streams' twists and bends. They build large, football-shaped nests of grass and mosses, often tucked on a rock ledge in midstream or behind a waterfall.

When and Where to See Them: In summer along swift, cold mountain streams particularly in northern mountains, moving into lowland hills and valleys in winter.

American Dipper

WESTERN BLUEBIRD

Sialia mexicana
Family: Thrushes
A.K.A.: California bluebird, chestnut-backed bluebird

Eye-catchers: The male's deep blue color, set off by his red breast, makes him a real crowd pleaser.

The male western bluebird is a deep blue with a rusty red breast and back and a whitish belly. The female is brownish gray with a wash of red on her breast and sides.

Natural History: While the mountain bluebird generally lives high in the mountains, the western bluebird brings its delightful show of avian color to lower-elevation woodlands and forest edges. But bluebirds aren't colorful and showy for our benefit. The male's blue color helps him attract a mate. Because the demand for nest cavities, which many bird species require, often exceeds supply, female bluebirds select mates who have appropriated a nest site. Once he has a house, the male puts on his Sunday best and advertises his home-ownership with a colorful display. Tail fanned and wings partially spread, he flutters and sings in front of the female. With a further solicitous show, he may land beside the female, preen her, and present her with bits of food.

Western bluebirds are bug eaters and frequently hunt from a low perch, looping out to catch insects fluttering near the ground. Sometimes they hover in the air above a prospective meal in the grass.

Like the eastern and mountain bluebirds, western bluebirds have been greatly affected by a loss of available nest cavities. Removal of dead trees, as well as the proliferation of aggressive non-native cavity-nesting birds like starlings and house sparrows, which invade bluebird territory and take over the nest sites, have greatly reduced nesting habitat for bluebirds. Construction of trails of bluebird nest boxes along country fence lines is helping bluebirds make a recovery.

When and Where to See Them: In summer in open mountain woodlands edging on open country, especially through the central part of the state, moving into lowland valleys, deserts, and coastal areas in central and southern California in winter.

Western Bluebird male   *Western Bluebird juvenile*

Western Bluebird female

MOUNTAIN BLUEBIRD

Sialia currucoides
Family: Thrushes
A.K.A.: Arctic bluebird, Rocky Mountain bluebird

Eye-catchers: The mountain bluebird looks like a scrap of the mountain sky made into a bird.

In the sunlight, the male bluebird is a striking azure blue with a paler breast. The female is gray with a bluish wash. In shadow, this bluebird is a dull gray.

Natural History: Bluebirds are one of the delights of the mountain summer, flitting across a mountain meadow like a bit of bright blue paper caught in the breeze. The color of the male is striking, seeming to defy nature. Indeed, the male's color is like a parlor trick; he does it with light and mirrors. The bird's blue plumage owes its color not to pigment but to the reflection of light from tiny structures on the feathers. The bluebird, in other words, is wearing a blue sequined suit. Turn off the lights and that flashy outfit fades to dull gray.

Mountain bluebirds prefer drier, more open habitat than other bluebirds. They nest in natural cavities and holes excavated by woodpeckers and will happily set up housekeeping in bluebird nest boxes at the edge of an open meadow. After settlement of the West and the extensive use of wooden posts for fencing, bluebirds also made use of holes in the posts for nests. With the removal of much standing dead timber and the replacement of old-time wooden fence posts with steel, much nesting habitat for bluebirds was lost and populations over much of the West declined. Fortunately, a mountain meadow without bluebirds was not something many westerners wanted to see. Determined efforts to provide artificial nest boxes for bluebirds in appropriate habitat are helping these beautiful birds make a comeback. Studies have found that bluebirds reared in artificial nest boxes prefer man-made boxes when they build nests of their own.

Bluebirds hunt in grassy meadows for insects, often hovering in the air like a helicopter before dropping down on prey in the grass. The abundance of bluebirds in a particular area may vary year to year depending upon height of the vegetation; they cannot see their prey if the grass is too long, as in wet years, and must go elsewhere.

When and Where to See Them: Mid-April to late September in open high mountain forests and valleys, primarily in central and northern California. Fall through spring in lowland open plains and farm fields.

Mountain Bluebird male

Mountain Bluebird female

AMERICAN ROBIN

Turdus migratorius
Family: Thrushes
A.K.A.: robin redbreast, migratory thrush

Eye-catchers: The robin's red breast is its legendary trademark.

This large, dark gray songbird has a bright "robin-red" breast and white eye ring. The female's breast is duller than the male's.

Natural History: This most familiar of songbirds needs little introduction. Robins have been memorialized in folklore and song as a symbol of the return of spring, which they announce with their *cheer-up, cheer-up* call. In some parts of the country they are the first bird to show up after a long, hard winter, often arriving while snow is still on the ground. This image is somewhat moot for California, since robins are year-round residents, with some intrastate movement from higher, colder summer locales to lowlands in winter. Robins remain a ubiquitous and prominent neighbor, but familiarity doesn't breed contempt. As comfortable as they are around humans, robins can be great fun to watch, and they offer us a peek at avian life. They often build their twiggy cup nests in trees in our yards. If we're lucky, we may watch them raise their young, poking worms and insects down the gaping mouths of their squalling babies. Later, like proud godparents, we watch as the spotted-breast babies take their first ungainly forays into the world of our backyard.

Even watching a robin hunt on the lawn is interesting. We may write them off as benign songbirds, but robins are actually predators, their prey being worms, insects, and other invertebrates. Contrary to popular belief, when a robin hops about your yard turning its head to the side, it isn't listening for worms but watching for movement in the grass. Robins hunt mainly by sight. Once prey is located they make a quick stab with their long, pointed bills, grabbing their earthworm prey as certainly as a hawk grabs a rabbit in its talons.

When and Where to See Them: Throughout the state year-round. In summer in mountain forests and suburbs of southern California, moving into lowland orchards, suburbs, parks, and gardens in winter.

American Robin male

American Robin juvenile

VARIED THRUSH

Ixoreus naevius
Family: Thrushes
A.K.A.: Pacific varied thrush, Oregon robin

Eye-catchers: The male varied thrush is boldly costumed in orange and slate blue.

The male is strikingly marked, with a blue gray back, tail, and nape, an orange throat and breast, orange wing bars, a black bar through the eye, and a bold black crescent across the breast. The female is dark gray instead of blue gray and generally more dull than the male, with a faint breast band.

Natural History: In the coastal forests of northern California, the varied thrush haunts the shaded forest floor, dressed like a jockey in boldly colored silks. Often keeping to the cover of rocks and undergrowth, it hunts for worms, grubs, insects, and other food. The varied thrush is also fond of mistletoe berries, and its genus name, *Ixoreus,* means "mistletoe-lover."

The varied thrush, like the robin, is a member of the thrush family, and its posture, appearance, and general behavior—scurrying around foraging for food— are reminiscent of the more familiar bird. But the varied thrush's world is very different from the suburban and woodland home of its robin cousin. In dense and dripping forests where the sense of the primeval hangs heavy, the voice of the hidden varied thrush sounds suddenly in a haunting, quavering whistle. Then silence, then another melancholy whistle that fades away among the trees before sounding again, the voice of a woodland sprite.

If you should miss seeing a varied thrush in its coastal forest habitat, and spotting it isn't easy in such an overgrown place, you may see one in the "off-season" as the birds disperse across California in winter, showing up in lowland coniferous forests, shaded ravines, cool watered canyons, and sometimes even parks, where they join robins in foraging for worms.

The **hermit thrush,** which looks a bit like a juvenile robin with its spotted breast, also inhabits forests. You are more likely to hear this shy thrush than see it, its remarkable bell-like song ringing out in phrases repeated at different pitches.

When and Where to See Them: In summer in humid northwestern coastal forests, moving into cool shaded woodlands, canyons, and dense forests through much of the state in winter.

Varied Thrush male

Hermit Thrush

WESTERN TANAGER

Piranga ludoviciana
Family: Tanagers
A.K.A.: Louisiana tanager

Eye-catchers: A spectacular flash of yellow, black, and red announces the male western tanager.

The male tanager is brightly colored, with a butter yellow body, red head, yellow wing bars, and black wings, back, and tail. The female is a drab olive yellow.

Natural History: "Look at that beautiful bird!" is the usual response to a first-time glimpse of a western tanager. Outfitted in blaze yellow, bright red, and black, the western tanager is a true eye-catcher.

Tanagers are summer visitors to midelevation coniferous and deciduous forests. Like Christmas ornaments they brighten up the green of the forest with a flash of bold color. Tanagers build fragile, saucer-shaped nests woven of grasses, bark, and weeds, usually placed in the fork of a tree branch up near the crown of the tree and far out from the trunk. The male sings readily, in a voice best described as sounding like a hoarse robin, his song carrying far through the woods. At the beginning of summer, tanagers feed on insects, including wasps, ants, caterpillars, and termites. They hunt the upper reaches of the forest canopy, often swooping out like flycatchers to catch flying insects, sometimes displaying impressive aerobatic prowess, darting among the branches or shooting straight up out of the top of a tree. Later in the summer, tanagers include berries and buds in their diet.

Though the western tanager is a bird of western forests, it is nicknamed "Louisiana tanager" in recognition of the fact it was first recorded by Meriwether Lewis of the Lewis and Clark expedition, which was exploring the Louisiana Purchase. Ironically, Lewis likely first sighted the bird somewhere in Idaho.

Brilliant color runs in the tanager family. The **summer tanager,** with its plumage like a brilliant red cloak, is found in some wooded areas of southern California and the southeastern deserts.

When and Where to See Them: In summer in open mountain forests of conifers and deciduous trees. During spring and fall migration in lowland wooded areas.

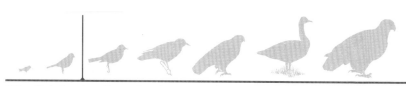

Western Tanager male   *Western Tanager female*

Summer Tanager male

WILSON'S WARBLER

Wilsonia pusilla
Family: Wood-warblers
A.K.A.: Wilson's blackcap, flycatching warbler, pileolated warbler

Eye-catchers: A busy scrap of yellow and olive flitting among streamside willows and topped with a bold, unmistakable cap of black is the male Wilson's warbler.

This bright little warbler is olive green on its back and wings and yellow underneath. The male has a prominent black cap; the female's cap is much more drab or even nonexistent.

Natural History: The Wilson's warbler flits in streamside thickets, bringing a bright spot of sunshine to the moist woodlands as its yellow breast flashes among the foliage. These warblers are generally easily visible because they aren't shy of humans and hunt the outside branches of shrubs and thickets instead of the upper canopy of tall trees. In typical warbler fashion, the Wilson's is a busy fellow, too busy to sit still and allow birdwatchers to get a long look at him. This handsome warbler is after insects, snapping them up as quick as can be. Sometimes the Wilson's warbler becomes excited, twitching like a second-grader on a church pew, flicking its tail frantically up and down, flipping its wings repeatedly, and rotating its tail in a circle. In keeping with its agitated pace, this warbler's song is equally frenetic, a rapid series of *chip, chip, chip* accelerating in tempo and becoming more insistent.

Like many of North America's nesting warblers, the Wilson's spends the cold months in the rain forests of Central America. Yet it chooses to nest in the high, cool forests of the north, its range spreading across northern Canada into Alaska. California is in the most southerly portion of its nesting range. Wilson's warblers build grassy, ball-shaped nests concealed on the ground or hidden in the lower branches of shrubs and thickets along lakes and streams. During migration, the Wilson's is one of the most common and abundant songbirds in California, passing the length of the state to northern nesting grounds.

Townsend's warbler, boldly marked in black and yellow, is another common and very handsome warbler that migrates through California.

When and Where to See Them: From mid-March to August in cool, moist riparian thickets and woodlands near water, through most of the state.

Wilson's Warbler male

Townsend's Warbler male in breeding plumage

BLACK-HEADED GROSBEAK

Pheucticus melanocephalus
Family: Finches
A.K.A.: Black-head, western grosbeak

Eye-catchers: The grosbeak's thick, stout bill stands out in a crowd.

This plump finch has a very heavy, pale bill. The male has a black head, robin red breast, black-and-white wings and tail, and yellow belly. The female is buffy with black streaks on the head and back and white stripes around the eyes.

Natural History: The name "grosbeak" is always a giveaway for this bird. Its bill is exaggeratedly thick and stout, creating a distinctive profile. Comparing the grosbeak's bill to those of other seed eaters is like comparing a sledgehammer to a hammer. When it comes to cracking open seeds, this tool is primo. Surprisingly, the grosbeak eats a varied diet ranging from heavy seeds to berries and insects.

The song of the black-headed grosbeak is rather like a robin's, though richer and more whistly, with trills as an added flourish. Once the male grosbeak arrives at its forest breeding grounds, he finds a perch and begins singing. The grosbeak's enthusiastic song fests have been known to go on for seven hours. But just sitting and singing is sometimes not enough, and the male will suddenly wing up into the air in front of the female, fanning wings and tail and singing with gusto, adding a showy song flight to his courtship repertoire. He may continue his musical flight show even as his mate incubates their eggs.

Though fairly secretive while nesting, grosbeaks are otherwise rather tame birds that come readily to feeders and will forage on the ground around campsites.

When and Where to See Them: Late March through September in riparian, mixed oak-conifer, and open coniferous woodlands mainly west of the Sierra Nevada and in southeastern deserts.

Black-headed Grosbeak male

DARK-EYED JUNCO

Junco hyemalis
Family: Finches
A.K.A.: Oregon junco, gray-headed junco, Oregon pink-sided junco, white-winged junco, slate-colored junco

Eye-catchers: You'll always recognize a junco by the smear of charcoal around the eye and the white tail edges visible when the bird flies.

There are four races of dark-eyed junco. The Oregon form has a dark, blue black cowl covering head and neck, a rusty back, rosy sides, and gray wings and tail. The gray-headed comes with light gray head and sides and rusty red back. The slate-colored is slate gray with a pale belly, and the white-winged is slate gray with white wing bars and white on the tail. A fifth junco, the pink-sided, is a phase of the Oregon form, with paler cowl and pink sides. All juncos have white tail edges visible in flight and dark coloring around the eye.

Natural History: The dark-eyed junco is one of those birds that stumps our human need to put neat boundaries around things and label them exactly. Presently, four different races or forms (dare we say "flavors"?), each with a different and distinct appearance, comprise the species known as dark-eyed junco. Each race looks like it should be a separate species, yet they interbreed, a situation that can drive crazy the people who officially classify birds into species. However juncos may be classified, these energetic, handsome, and easily seen birds, who adapt well to life around humans, are a pleasure to watch.

All four junco races inhabit California, but the Oregon and gray-headed are the ones most likely to be seen here. Most common by far is the Oregon form, with its handsome black cowl covering head and neck ("junco" is a term for the hood of an executioner). Gray-headed juncos, with a back the color of a robin's breast, also breed in the state. The slate-colored and white-winged appear only occasionally.

Juncos are a common and familiar summer bird of mountain forests. Like humans, they seek the cool of high altitudes in summer, moving back to lowland areas when the weather turns cold, showing up in parks and backyards, where they happily come to feeders for seed. Though seed-eaters, juncos are ground-feeding birds that forage for spilled seed beneath hanging feeders rather

Dark-eyed Junco male

than perching on them. They readily use platform or tray feeders and sometimes gather in large numbers. In late winter and early spring the flocks follow the emergence of buds and ripening of seeds back up into higher-elevation nesting grounds where they break up into pairs to nest and rear their young. At this time they supplement their seed diet with insects.

Juncos build soft cup nests woven of grasses and sheltered in a depression on the ground beneath a shrub or overhang. Once the young are out of the nest, the junco family joins others of its kind in large flocks. Spreading out in foraging groups, the birds keep in contact with each other via constant cheeps and calls.

When and Where to See Them: In summer in mountain forests moving to lowland woodlands, chaparral, parks, gardens, and open areas in winter.

RED CROSSBILL

Loxia curvirostra
Family: Finches
A.K.A.: American crossbill

Eye-catchers: Look closely at the bizarre crossed bill of the crossbill and you can mistake it for no other bird.

The male is a bright brick red with dusky wings and tail, and the female is dusky with a yellowish wash and dark wings and tail. Both have a twisted bill, with the tip of the upper mandible bent over and down and the lower mandible bent up.

Natural History: Birds have evolved all sorts of adaptive tools to help them in their particular lifestyles, and the beak of the crossbill is one of the screwiest examples (pun intended). Bend your index finger over your thumb and you have an idea of what the crossbill's unique beak looks like. The upper and lower mandibles are twisted so they bend one over the other. This isn't some goofy mutation but a specialized adaptation for prying the nuts out of pine cones, sort of a bird-beak can opener. With the cone scales held apart by its twisted bill, the bird then picks the seeds out with its tongue. Individual birds are either "right-handed" or "left-handed" depending upon which way their bill is bent. Baby crossbills hatch with "normal" beaks, their bills gradually crossing in the weeks after they fledge.

Crossbills are so specialized for feeding on pine nuts that their migration patterns mirror the cone crops. A site they wintered in one year may have no crossbills the next year as the birds spread farther afield to find food. An abundant cone crop one year, which fostered the hatching of increased numbers of chicks, may be followed by an "irruption," or outward migration, as the large population must spread farther to find enough food. Because many crossbills spend the winter in high-altitude and northern forests, they have a special pouch in their throat that allows them to store seeds to feed on to get them through a cold night, enabling them to have a sort of bird's midnight snack.

When and Where to See Them: Irregularly in coniferous mountain forests year-round, moving occasionally in winter into lowland areas—orchards, parks, ranches, coastal forests, and deserts.

Red Crossbill male

Red Crossbill female

RECOMMENDED READING

A Birder's Guide to Southern California. Brad Schram. Colorado Springs, Colo.: American Birding Association. 1998.

An Introduction to Northern California Birds. Herbert Clarke. Missoula, Mont.: Mountain Press Publishing Company. 1995.

An Introduction to Southern California Birds. Herbert Clarke. Missoula, Mont.: Mountain Press Publishing Company. 1989.

An Island Called California. Elna Bakker. Berkeley and Los Angeles: University of California Press. 1982.

Birder's Guide to Northern California. LoLo and Jim Westrich. Houston: Gulf Publishing Company. 1991.

California Birds: Their Status and Distribution. Arnold Small. Vista, Calif.: Ibis Publishing Company. 1994.

California Wildlife Viewing Guide. Jeanne L. Clark. Helena, Mont.: Falcon Press. 1992.

CALIFORNIA'S BIRDING HOT SPOTS

California is unparalleled in the lower 48 states for its diversity of habitats and bird species. Great birding locales are found the length of the state, many of them readily accessible. The following list of birding locations is only the tip of the iceberg for California birdwatching opportunities. For detailed information and specific directions to these sites and others, consult *A Birder's Guide to Southern California* and *Birder's Guide to Northern California* (see the Recommended Reading list). These and many other birding and natural history books are available from the Los Angeles Audubon Society Bookstore, 7377 Santa Monica Boulevard, West Hollywood, CA 90046.

Southern California

Salton Sea and vicinity, including Salton Sea National Wildlife Refuge and Wister Unit of State Imperial Wildlife Area—*waterfowl, wading and shorebirds, cranes, desert birds, gulls, pelicans.*

Anza-Borrego Desert State Park—*desert birds, hummingbirds, owls.*

Mission Bay, San Diego—*waterfowl, wading birds, gulls, terns.*

Point Loma—*migrant land birds, especially vagrants.*

Tijuana Slough National Wildlife Refuge—*migrant land birds, wading and shorebirds.*

South San Diego Bay—*wading and shorebirds, terns, gulls, marsh birds.*

Malibu Lagoon—*waterfowl, wading and shorebirds, gulls, terns, cormorants.*

Bolsa Chica and Upper Newport Bay—*waterfowl, wading and shorebirds, terns, gulls, grebes, rails, marsh birds.*

Angeles Crest National Forest—*mountain birds.*

Santa Barbara oceanfront and University of California campus—*shorebirds, waterfowl, gulls, terns, migrants.*

McGrath Beach State Park, Ventura County—*shorebirds, waterfowl, gulls, terns, migrants.*

Morro Bay—*coastal rock birds, loons, cormorants, marsh birds, pelicans, waterfowl.*

Northern California

Monterey Bay and Peninsula, including the oceanfront, Moss Landing, Point Pinos, Carmel River mouth, and Point Lobos. *Ocean birds, marsh birds, wading and shorebirds, gulls, terns, grebes, cormorants, rock birds, sea and land migrants, and raptors.*

Bolinas Lagoon—*waterfowl, wading and shorebirds, marsh birds.*

Palo Alto Baylands Reserve—*rails, waterbirds, marsh birds.*

Point Reyes—*hawks, migrating land birds, ocean birds, birds of rocky habitats and open fields.*

Lake Tahoe, including El Dorado National Forest, Emerald Bay State Park, and China Flat. *Eagles and hawks, woodpeckers, hummingbirds, owls, and a variety of passerines including jays, kinglets, grosbeaks, warblers, finches, nuthatches.*

Mono Basin—*grouse, gulls, phalaropes, grebes, shorebirds, waterfowl, woodpeckers, flycatchers, raptors, magpies.*

Sacramento Valley National Wildlife Refuges—*waterfowl, especially geese in tremendous numbers in fall and winter, cranes, raptors, marsh birds.*

Lower Klamath and Tule Lake National Wildlife Refuges—*hundreds of bald eagles in winter, thousands of waterfowl and shorebirds in migration and nesting.*

The following national parks offer good birding and good public access. Their visitor centers offer nature programs, bird lists, information and books on local birds, and are staffed by knowledgeable people available to give up-to-the-minute information on local birding opportunities:

Yosemite National Park

Redwood National Park

Joshua Tree National Park

Point Reyes National Seashore

Lassen National Park

Sequoia National Park

Kings Canyon National Park

INDEX

About the Author

Mary Taylor Gray is a professional nature writer specializing in birdwatching and wildlife viewing. A biologist with a degree in zoology, she is author of six books, including *Watchable Birds of the Southwest, Watchable Birds of the Rocky Mountains,* and *The Guide to Colorado Birds.* She writes articles for such publications as *Birder's World, Birdwatcher's Digest,* and *Outside* and a monthly column on birdwatching for Denver's *Rocky Mountain News.* California's diversity of birds and habitats frequently draws Mary west from her home in Denver, which she shares with her husband, Richard Young, and daughter, Olivia.

Mary Taylor Gray and daughter Olivia. —RICK YOUNG PHOTO

About the Photographer

An avid birder since childhood, Herbert Clarke has studied birds all over the world, with special emphasis on California. He is the author of *An Introduction to Southern California Birds* and *An Introduction to Northern California Birds,* and coauthor of *Birds of the West.* His writings and photographs have appeared in many books and natural history publications. Mr. Clarke makes his home in Glendale, California, with his wife and constant field companion, Olga.

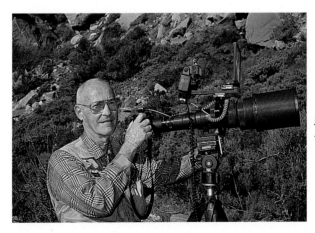

Herbert Clarke
—OLGA CLARKE PHOTO

We encourage you to patronize your local bookstores. Most stores will order any title that they do not stock. You may also order directly from Mountain Press by mail, using the order form provided below, or by calling our toll-free number and using your Visa or MasterCard. We will gladly send you a complete catalog upon request.

Some other Natural History titles of interest:

____An Introduction to Northern California Birds	$14.00
____An Introduction to Southern California Birds	$14.00
____Birds of the Central Rockies	$14.00
____Birds of the Pacific Northwest Mountains	$14.00
____Desert Wildflowers of North America	$24.00
____Geology Underfoot in Death Valley and Owens Valley	$16.00
____Geology Underfoot in Southern California	$14.00
____OWLS Whoo are they?	$12.00
____Roadside Geology of Northern California	$15.00
____Roadside History of California	paper $18.00 / cloth $30.00
____Roadside Plants of Southern California	$15.00
____Sierra Nevada Wildflowers	$16.00
____Watchable Birds of the Rocky Mountains	$14.00
____Watchable Birds of the Southwest	$14.00

Please include $3.00 per order to cover shipping and handling.

Send the books marked above. I enclose $_____

Name_____

Address_____

City_____State_____Zip_____

☐ Payment enclosed (check or money order in U.S. funds)

Bill my: ☐ VISA ☐ MasterCard Expiration Date:_____

Card No._____

Signature _____

MOUNTAIN PRESS PUBLISHING COMPANY
P. O. Box 2399 • Missoula, MT 59806
Order Toll Free **1-800-234-5308**
Have your Visa or MasterCard ready.